OUR FINITE BOUNTY

An Anthology of Sustainability Topics

Edited by Yolanda Romero and Roy Vũ
North Lake College

Kendall Hunt
publishing company

This book is printed on sustainable certified paper based on the U.S. Forest Stewardship Council standards.

Cover image: Village Landscape 2 - Pressed Leaves and Flowers, Corn Husk and Rose Petals on Paper. Courtesy of Pavlina Panova

Artist Statement: My art is a symbiosis of the cultural heritage I came with from Bulgaria and my new life in America as an artist.

My main medium is pressed leaves, but I also use a wide variety of natural materials such as flowers, seeds, fruit and veggie peels, and herbs. Nature gives me the materials to work with and inspires me with its creative power and beauty. It has been challenging to preserve the colors, shapes, and textures of the materials that Nature creates and at the same time so rewarding to give a new life to these materials through my art. A new direction of my art is combining clay reliefs and pressed leaves.

I believe in the transforming power of art and its ability to make people better and more spiritual. As an environmental artist and a teacher, I work for a new perception and appreciation of Nature.

Pavlina Panova
Pavlina Panova was born in 1959 in Bulgaria, where she had a successful career as a published author, literary critic, and teacher in Bulgarian Language and Literature.

In 1999, she and her family came to America and since then they have been living in Irving, Texas. Soon after her arrival, she enrolled as an English as a Second Language student at North Lake College. At the same time, she started creating small pictures with pressed leaves and became passionately involved in this new artistic way of expression. After a few years of experimenting with pressed leaves and other natural materials, she realized that she needed more knowledge for developing her style. In 2007, she went back to North Lake College as a full-time credit student majoring in Art and English. She gained not only practical skills, but also theoretical knowledge that has influenced her work tremendously. Since then she has been transforming and applying different techniques in her work with pressed leaves. For the last few years, she has been actively working in a new direction of combining clay reliefs and leaves. In 2011, she graduated with Associate's degree in Art. In 2013, Pavlina started teaching Pressed Leaves and Flowers Class and Clay Jewelry Class at North Lake College. She has been a guest speaker for Sustainability Program at North Lake College.

Kendall Hunt
publishing company

www.kendallhunt.com
Send all inquiries to:
4050 Westmark Drive
Dubuque, IA 52004-1840

Published in the United States of America

Photo courtesy of Candace Eldridge and Sammy Romero.

In loving memory of Dr. Yolanda Garcia Romero
(1951–2016)

Contents

Introduction

Sustainability intersects our lives more often than we realize or admit. Economic, environmental, and societal sustainability encompass economic equality, environmental justice, and the social construct of a community. Within the three tenets of sustainability, the human race perpetually seeks ways to improve our own personal health, determine how we travel, amplify social justice, mark our unique identity, encourage peace and unity, and develop and protect the most valued and sacred resources of our respective global societies. Consequently, human capital becomes the most precious resource, as we attempt to meet our current living needs without so much sacrificing the needs of the future.

In these 11 essays, we cover more ground on societal sustainability, particularly in the Mexican immigrant and Vietnamese diasporic communities of the United States. In future editions, we hope to expand our coverage of the economic and environmental tenets of sustainability. Nevertheless, we must begin somewhere—somewhere familiar, yet an outlier to most.

When we first shared our ideas for this project, Dr. Yolanda Garcia Romero was still alive and well. Dr. Romero was my mentor, colleague, and dearest friend at North Lake College. On Friday mid-mornings, we sat in the campus cafeteria and exchanged our thoughts and discussed our plans for the book. We mapped our ideas on how to incorporate sustainability topics via original essays. We discovered that, quite naturally, our research interests in critical immigration and refugee studies pertain to societal sustainability. To make our anthology more interesting and expansive for our students, we announced a "Call for Papers (CFP)" to invite our colleagues to submit abstract proposals for our collection of essays on a variety of sustainability topics. Needless to say, we were excited and waited with much anticipation for what we may read and learn from our colleagues' submissions. We publicized our CFP in October 2015 and looked forward to collecting and perusing the submitted abstracts.

It was late December 2015, just two days before our college campus would close for the winter break. Christmas was right around the corner when Sammy, Dr. Romero's loving husband, broke the news to me: "Yolanda has cancer of the liver." Our voices cracked a few times over the phone as we tried to hold our emotions throughout the conversation. When Sammy said goodbye, the news of Dr. Romero's terminal cancer broke my heart. A Chekhovian winter has settled in for the duration of her life—we all hoped for the best, but knew that it would be extremely difficult to overcome this fate.

Less than eight months later, Dr. Romero, despite her valiant and courageous battle with a terminal illness, took her last breath. She had an indomitable spirit, and left behind a legacy in academia, the Irving community, and our college. With less than a 48-hour notice, personal testimonies from former and current students, friends, colleagues, neighbors, relatives, and family members across the nation poured in by the hundreds, as they attended her memorial at North Lake. The somber yet memorable scenery left an indelible and permanent mark in many minds and hearts. Dr. Romero's life was celebrated and remembered fondly. She inspired all of us who appeared at her memorial, wake, or funeral. She was an academic pioneer and legend, as well as an accomplished scholar and inspirational teacher and mentor for her peers and students. Dr. Romero had accomplished so much in 65 years on earth, living a glorious life replete with remarkable achievements and deserving accolades.

Since the cancer took away our brightest star so suddenly for many us, Dr. Romero left another legacy: her unfinished works that originated from her incredible mind. When news of her cancer broke our spirits, our collaborative projects, including the sustainability anthology, that remained a shiny and exciting scholarly venture before that fateful December day, lost great momentum and traction. The anthology remained mostly idle throughout her courageous struggle with liver cancer. When she left us in August 2016, I was unsure if our co-edited anthology would ever surface.

Then, a couple of unique occurrences settled in after Dr. Romero's funeral. Although we were acquainted before, Ngọc, my wife, and I struck a beautiful friendship with Sammy that continues to blossom and grow, as we have a penchant to exchange stories of Dr. Romero. The second occurrence became rather a new dawning. That is, our co-edited book project started to gain some footing and gradually came into focus. A few of my colleagues and I rallied around the idea of not only pushing the project forward, but also retaining Dr. Romero's name as a coeditor. In other words, her memory, spirit, and legacy have endured and sustained us to continue and complete this unfinished work. Her name would live on, we declared, and so we returned to the work that she did not have an opportunity to complete. This anthology, hopefully, will add to Dr. Romero's growing legacy. And so, her name remains, and her spirit endures.

In this collection of sustainability topics, we included some of Dr. Romero's previously published essays, as well as a new, unpublished one—one that she presented at the Spring 2016 East Texas Historical Association Conference; it was her final academic presentation. This anthology also includes contributions from Dr. Brett Bodily, James Duran, Brandon Morton, and Dr. Roy Vũ.

The first essay, "Revolution and Community Building in the Mexican Descent Community, 1900–1930" by Dr. Romero, demonstrates the struggles of Mexicans as they fled from the violence of the Mexican Revolution and migrated to the United States in hopes of sustaining their culture and communities, as they created new beginnings. In Dr. Bodily's autobiographical essay, "Blue Milk," he harkens back to his childhood experience with drinking powdered, blue milk, tracing its historical phenomenon, and recalls his transformative experience with raw milk. In Dr. Romero's next essay, "Self-Help, Cooperation, and Community Sustainability," she analyzes the importance of mutual aid societies in Mexican American communities in the midst of racial discrimination and how they used to meet their social needs, including proper funeral burials.

In "Southern Vietnamese Nationalism as Analogous to a Nurse Log," the author compares the rise of Southern Vietnamese nationalism from the Cold War ashes to stoke and nurture the Vietnamese American communities, similar to a fallen, decomposed tree that provides essential nutrients to new growth. In Dr. Romero's third essay, "March of Faith," she provides a first-hand account of Mexican American activists in Lubbock, Texas, and their march for social equality and justice in 1971. In Brandon Morton's essay, "Generation Monarch: Pathways of Migration in the Twenty-First

Century," the author emphasizes the significance of the monarch butterfly and explains how humans have devastated its population and yet still have an opportunity to restore and sustain the butterfly's population, and in turn, improve our agricultural food system.

In "A Double Home Loss? The Invisible Space of Little Sài Gòn in Midtown Houston," Dr. Vũ discusses the rise and decline of a once-thriving Vietnamese American business district that became gentrified, disappearing into an invisible ethnic space and a double home loss for Vietnamese Houstonians. In Dr. Romero's fourth essay, "*Adelante Compañeros:* The Sanitation Worker's Struggle in Lubbock, Texas, 1968–1972," the author discusses the sanitation workers and their daily struggles, as well as the support they received from the local Mexican descent community. In Prof. Duran's essay, "Out of the Car and Into the Future," the author addresses the impact of bicycles as a sustainable mode of transportation, particularly in urban settings where two-wheeled travel could dramatically improve not only our personal health, but also our environs in a plethora of ways.

In "Farm to Freedom: In Our Garden, After the War," Dr. Vũ focuses on the nurturing effects of home gardens and how they heal the physical health and mental well-being, as well as help retain the identity of a populace traumatized by war, refuge, and resettlement. Finally, we appropriately end the anthology with Dr. Romero's last essay, "We Are Not All Mexicans: The Growth of the Latino Population in Irving, Texas, 1970–2000." Here, she examines the diverse and rich history of the Latino population in Irving, Texas, and the significant cultural contributions they have made with their stories and communities.

These 11 essays reinforce the importance of the inclusivity and maintenance of all three components of sustainability: economic, environmental, and societal. The aforementioned tenets of sustainability are evident and ubiquitous in human history. To further sustain our world with social justice, economic stability and interdependence, and environmental improvements, the current and future generations would best be served by acknowledging, adhering, and practicing sustainable measures that would facilitate the endurance of the human race and spirit. Though we currently have a finite bounty to consume and live, the recently born and unborn generations remain our most precious resource. Therefore, we have a duty to bestow our most precious resource with the greatest opportunity to make our given bounty less finite for all.

REVOLUTION AND COMMUNITY BUILDING IN THE MEXICAN DESCENT COMMUNITY, 1900–1930

Yolanda Romero

When the Revolution began, Mexicans crossing the Texas–Mexico border acquired employment and many moved north with railroad and agricultural industries to the developing areas of Texas. In Texas, Mexican immigrants joined Mexican Americans already there struggling to improve their pecuniary conditions. Like the Mexican Americans, these Spanish-speaking people began experiencing life in the labor camps and segregated areas of towns and cities in the region, sharing their cultural traditions and vulnerable situation.

Tirso Dominguez who fought first with Pancho Villa and then became a *Carrancista* found a home in Slaton, less than 20 miles from Lubbock during the Mexican Revolution. Dominguez was born on January 28, 1900, in Parral, Chihuahua, where he grew up. He was with Pancho Villa until attempting to jump the train at Celaya. However, he lost his step and had to hold on to a window all the way to Aguas Calientes. In Aguas Calientes, he joined the Carranza military because he "could never get along with the Villistas." In order to join the Carranza army, Tirso stole a man's horse. Tirso remembered that the man woke up and dressed in nothing but his underwear ran outside to stop the theft. Scared, with no recourse, Tirso fought the man and was forced to choke him to death to stop him from waking his neighbors. His highest rank in both the Villa army and Carranza military was that of Captain. Dominguez married his wife in May of 1923 and came to the United States. Tirso was 23 years of age and his wife was 17 when they moved to Northwest Texas. There were six other Mexican descent families living in Slaton. In 1925, Tirso began working for the railroad and became a leader in the community, until he retired in the late 1970s. Angie Aguilar Todd who lived in Slaton as a girl recollected that in the 1940s her sister was a *reyna* (queen) and she the *India bonita* (pretty Indian girl) at *fiestas* Dominguez had helped to organize.

Traditional Mexican holidays and ceremonies celebrated then and now were *el Diez y seis de Septiembre* (September 16), *Cinco de Mayo* (May 5), *quinceañeras* (15-year-old's parties), and *bailes caseros* (house dances). *Compadrazgo* was also an important institution to these Hispanics. *El Diez y seis de Septiembre* is celebrated in Mexico. It marks the day in 1810 when Father Hidalgo began the Independence movement against Spain's power. The battle for Independence lasted until 1821. Mexican Independence is celebrated throughout Texas with parades, fiestas, dances, and *senorita* or *reyna* contests. In the early years, the celebration was more of a neighborhood event with a *jamaica* (small fair) held outside at a central location such as the church. Small booths were set up to sell food such as tamales, tripas, or menudo. An outside dance and *bailes folkloricos* or mariachis were usually part of the September 16 festivities and *reyna* or *senorita* was chosen to reign over the Fiestas Patrias. *Cinco de Mayo* celebrated the defeat of the French in 1861. This event is celebrated much like the September 16 festivities, although festivities are not as impressive. A *quinceañera* is a special event in the life of a Mexican descent woman. It symbolizes the young adolescent becoming a woman. The young woman's 15th birthday is celebrated with a special mass with *padrinos* (godparents) as well as a dinner and dance for relatives and friends. *Quinceañeras* are popular events in the Mexican American community and are celebrated in the Mexican tradition. Godparents play a significant role in *quinceañeras*, baptismals, confirmations, and weddings. The parents of the child or young man or woman are *compadres* to the *padrinos*. *Compadrazgo* develops a kinship among families that aids in strengthening cultural traditions. Texas experienced its first wave of Mexicans joining Mexican Americans during the first three decades of the twentieth century. At that time, the first *barrios* began to develop where migrant workers came to work. Missions and then churches were established by the Catholic Church in these areas. But Hispanics were still perceived as transients although their neighborhoods were growing and becoming well-established communities.

BLUE MILK

Brett H. Bodily

On the way to buy blue milk, I saw Elsie's face stretched broadly across a roadside billboard. She was the "poster cow" of the dairy industry, adorned by an ambrosial smile, petite horns, and an indelible rosary of yellow daisies. Her eyes glanced at a neighboring milk depot, beckoning and directing thirsty travelers toward her company's "perfect dairy product." Despite the fact that my father called our destination "a dairy," it didn't look like dairies I had seen on TV or in books at school, nor did it look anything like the dairy located next door to my grandparents' home in California. Elsie's industrial facility was metallic white, constructed of metal and concrete, bouncing Arizona's blazing sun into my squinting eyes. I scanned the premises. There were no alfalfa fields surrounding the complex; not a single tree, shrub, or plant adorned the facility—nothing to shade us from the heat as we walked across the pavement. We entered the warehouse through glass doors and traveled a few steps toward a service counter and exchanged glances with a middle-aged man wearing a western plaid shirt.

Where is Elsie? I wondered, peeking over the worn *Formica* countertop, my head bobbing up and down, my eyes searching for a small glimpse of her dazzling complexion, but I didn't see a single cow.

"Workin' hard or hardly workin'?" my dad asked the man standing behind the counter.

The man chuckled and then asked, "What can I do you out of?"

My dad didn't need to peruse the chalkboard marquee located on the wall behind our clerk. He obviously knew what he wanted.

"Fifty pound milk," he responded, reaching for his wallet. "Half price today, right?"

"Yeah, when pigs fly!" the man said with a smirk and a piercing glance over his reading glasses.

Our attendant began forcefully pressing keys on his gray-colored cash register, the kind that displayed white, rotating numbers through a small glass window. His fingers danced on the keyboard until his pinky pressed the total key, seemingly playing the last note of a composition in a slightly different timbre. His hand lifted gently in the air as he announced, "nine ninety-five please." My dad handed him a couple of bills, and the clerk continued playing the register keys as numbers appeared, rolled, and appeared again through the small glass window. He paused, and once again played that final key, except this time a bell rang and the register tray popped out and bounced off the man's protruding belly. In one choreographed motion, he gracefully placed my dad's bills into the register's tray and swept a nickel from the coin slot, leaned forward, closing the tray with his belly button, and tore off the paper receipt, handing it to my father with a smile. We stood silently, not sure if we were supposed to applaud.

"Fifty milk!" the man said, stooping while pressing a button on a cylinder microphone located next to his cash register.

A few moments later, two flexible plastic doors, located near the end of the counter, began to move. I watched a short, stocky man, soaked with sweat, emerge with a sack over his left shoulder. He carefully navigated the counter's edge in order to set our order on the floor, sending small puffs of white dust into the air. I was too young to read the words on the bag, but Elsie's black and white picture said everything, and it was at this moment I began to understand where blue milk originated.

The so-called "milk" came in a pure white paper bag, the same type of bag used for chicken feed, too large for me to wrap my arms around and obviously too heavy for me to carry by myself, but I helpfully hefted a corner on the way to the car. On the bag, Elsie seemed to smile at me. She looked so human. I imaged her and other brown cows grinning warmly as they stood for milking, wearing floral garlands, halos of yellow daisies draped around their necks, winking long eyelashes at me as they stood blissfully for milking while humming pleasant tunes. Of course, Borden's marketing department had something to do with my effervescent imagination.

On the next morning, my mother mixed a usual batch of "powdered milk"—as my parents called it. All she had to do was scoop one part powder from the sack and three parts water from the tap and *voilà*, we had milk. Despite the fact that I had been drinking this stuff for longer than I could remember, and I never really thought much about its bluish color, I couldn't help but sense an overwhelming feeling of culinary consciousness rise within me. I peeked inside my cup, *really* noticing the peculiar blue tint. The dustiness of the liquid filled my nose, and my taste buds sensed a hint of dairy essence masked by chlorine. After I swallowed, millions of tiny gritty grains lingered on my tongue, leaving very little to appreciate and even less to desire.

What were my parents doing to me? I thought to myself, unaware that over 100 years had passed since the first blue milk began squirting into dirty milk pales, endangering the lives of naïve dairy lovers like me. Somehow, I felt an affinity for New Yorkers of the late nineteenth century, a time when whiskey brewers discovered the bovine's proclivity for distillery waste. Who would have imagined cows could produce so much milk on distillery by-products? Brewers did, but the blue tint caught them by surprise. Much to their chagrin, a few revealing articles in *The New York Times* exposed their scams. One lengthy article published in October 1884 touted, "A MENACE TO HEALTH AND LIFE IN THE CITY—HOW ANIMALS ARE FATTENED—THE BREWERS' LARGE PROFITS." Activists pushed, but clever food engineers were one step ahead, thinning their milk with water in order to boost revenues, thickening their milk with eggs while adding molasses in order to shroud the watery consistency and taste. What about the odd color? Staring into my cup, I could only imagine how these genius dairymen quickly began whitewashing blue milk with starch, flour, chalk, plaster of Paris, and who knows what else in order to cover the bluish tint, a seemingly unbelievable story until I read Ron Schmid's *The Untold Story of Milk*.

Schmid explains how distillery dairymen got away with the scam because engineered distillery milk seemed to look, feel, and taste like authentic Orange County milk from New York, a popular, regional milk crafted from pastured cows feeding on lush clover and timothy grass, giving the milk a white yet slightly yellowish color, creamy texture, and subtly sweet taste. Tipsy brewery cows, on the other hand, were only slightly inconvenient to manage, especially when they were packed into small pens, side to side, wall to wall. In a way, they helped prop each other up; besides, milk was selling just as well if not better than spirits, so it was economic genius—well, until blue milk began infecting infants with tuberculosis, diphtheria, diarrhea, and other diseases.

As food historians argue, science saved industrial milk. The discovery of harmful pathogens, smaller than the eye could see, swimming in fresh milk, led to a revolution: pasteurization. But what about me, the kid in the twentieth century? Well, I was safer than the New Yorkers of the 1800s because my blue milk was not only pasteurized but dried: "double protection." At least that is what the guy at the depot said. I guess this was a blessing.

I was born of parents raised in the protofeminist, industrialized food era, a time presumably created to free women from endless domestication, a time when food could be adulterated into a cheap, convenient form. We lived the "American Dream," dining on modern marvels of science and technology: frozen pizza, Velveeta, and Salisbury steak TV dinners. As my mother knew well, canned vegetables were easy to purchase, store, and serve. Frozen foods were temptingly simple to prepare. Margarine was much cheaper than butter, and my mother didn't need to spend time working real butter into a pie crust when vegetable shortening ensured a flaky crust in minutes.

Growing up in the 1970s, I didn't know that surplus weapon materials, government funding, and exploding technology generated a new way of eating as bombs became fertilizer for farmland desperately needing to recover from the dust bowl of the 1930s. Science promised to nourish depleted soils, stop erosion, increase productivity, and meet the demands of an increasing population of hungry baby boomers. Sweet corn hybrids were emerging and reducing meat costs, high-fructose corn syrup was becoming a major ingredient in everything, and our legislators were working hard on government farm subsidies in order to reduce food production costs—predominantly for processed, convenience foods and meat products. Amid all this, most important to my mom and dad, industrialization promised a lot of "food" for a lot less money. I was doomed to drink blue milk for many years.

In my pubescent years, adults used to say children perpetuated their parents' behaviors, sometimes exponentially, which meant, as I entered adulthood, I should have indulged myself in blue milk. But I believed in outliers—like the shy kid who grew up to stand in front of millions of buyers at global tech conferences, and the kid who refused vegetables and grew up to passionately launch an award-winning vegetarian food blog. For me, the possibility of tasting real milk came in my mid-thirties. Perhaps, I was coming of age or feeling post-modern or just experiencing an early midlife crisis; whatever the case, sitting in front of my computer one evening, shrouded by darkness, I dared type the words "raw milk" into my search engine. I looked left and right as though someone was watching me, discovering my clandestine motives.

A few days later, entering a local artisan cheese shop's address into my GPS, I pointed my car and a few friends toward the countryside near Dublin, Texas. I eventually exited the freeway, pulled onto a dirt driveway, passed a sign displaying a cartoon cheesemaker stirring a large vat of milk, a blonde and husky man with a demure smile, working over the caption, "Made by hand, blessed by God." We made our way to a small, red-colored building situated in front of a large metal barn housing tractors and various implements. This quaint little façade, accented by a small, covered porch with two wooden rocking chairs and a reposing Great Pyrenees, obviously retired, appeared to be the place. It looked more like a country cafe than a cheese shop, but what did we know; we were just city folks trying to get a taste of the country, a taste of real food.

Exiting the car, I stretched my legs, having driven about two and a half hours from the suburbs of Dallas, admired the campestral scenery, and breathed in rich cow manure conveying on a gentle breeze. Hesitantly approaching the front door of the cheese shop, glancing at one another, waiting for someone to take the lead, we saw the curtains move. Stewart, the cheesemaker, obviously the corporeal image of the cartoon man on the sign we passed, pressed his fair complexion and blondish gray-haired head against one of the window panes and waved, inviting us warmly into his world, a world of artisan cave-aged cheddar. Laying out samples across a granite countertop, he began explaining the process: milking, heating, stirring, molding, and aging. With each creamy morsel, my senses danced with delight—the tastes were foreign yet somewhat familiar, lost and then found.

"Have you ever had raw milk?" Stewart interrupted.

We looked at one another and then inaudibly shook our heads in short, negative gesticulations. "Well, let me give you some," he said as he boldly turned, reaching for the nearest, unmarked plastic jug shelved in his cooler and began pouring several small *Dixie* cups of a slightly yellow-colored liquid. I stared at the small paper cups decorated with floral print. This was the moment I was waiting for. My hand boldly reached for a cup when suddenly a rush of voices flooded my mind: *It's not pasteurized. What about pathogens? You could get sick. You could die!* Everything the media had told me, the food industry had told me, and the man who sold my parents blue milk at Elsie's depot had told me entered the stage of my imagination. Flashes of my family's old television set displaying images of Jim Jones' disciples laying in masses, dead, surrounded by small cups flashed across my memory. I smirked, took the cup, brought the paper to my lips, flirtatiously breathing in a cool, slightly grassy effervescence, and sipped as Stewart watched me like a mischievous child. I defiantly swallowed.

Grumblings, nausea, vomiting, death?

None of the sort, of course.

"Good, huh?" Stewart asked, lifting his blonde eyebrows and bobbing his head. Forcing a precocious smile, I pressed my tongue against my front teeth, pulled it back, and basked in a clean and creamy aftertaste, a full, rich flavor—nothing gritty, nothing bitter. I swallowed again, and again, until the cup was empty. I asked for another sample; Stewart obliged, and I drank again, searching for the watery taste, gritty texture, and the powdery essence, but only cool, thick sensations lingered, coating my stomach, soothing my skepticism, and awakening my body to the world of real milk, creamier and more flavorful. Needless to say, I bought 120 dollars' worth of dairy products that day: several pounds of artisan cheeses, a quart of yogurt, half gallon of cream, and five gallons of raw milk, none of it was blue.

SELF-HELP, COOPERATION, AND COMMUNITY SUSTAINABILITY

Yolanda Romero

Mutual aid societies were common throughout the country including the Southwest during the late nineteenth to early twentieth century in all immigrant communities. The Mexican descent community was no different. These societies emphasized cooperation to support their members by sharing resources to not only minimize interaction with the dominant culture but also alleviate stress on the affected family. In Lubbock, Texas, the *Socios del Cementerio* (The Cemetery Society) was not politically motivated and simply acted as a support network. It was organized in 1926 by the leaders of the *barrio* residents who paid $2.50 a year to be members of this society. There was no limit to the number of family members buried a year for this fee. *Los Socios* purchased an acre of land with only members paying toward the membership fee allowed to be buried on the land. There was also a clause that allowed the burial of migrant workers without family. Any money collected from new members would be used for maintaining the cemetery. Under no circumstances did the city or county help with the upkeep of this section. The construction of caskets was redistributed every six months among the members. The women were responsible for helping with the wake, which at the time would have been held in someone's home. The music, flowers, and the rosary were also the responsibility of the members. The grieving family was not to be burdened with details.

The association was organized around a board of three members, the president, vice president, and secretary, known as the *Direction*, who met once a month to discuss any related matters to the society. Visits to the cemetery indicated that *Los Socios* used traditional wooden crosses, small concrete headstones, and inscriptions that were for the most part written in Spanish. Members opened and closed the grave sites and shared the maintenance of grounds on their acre of land. These services were provided by *Los Socios* to members to avoid the $5.00 cost of opening and closing graves (1925–1935) in addition to the $15.00 charge for burial plots. This acre of land became known as the "old Catholic section."

References

Daniel Albidrez Papers, Microfilmed Collection, Southwest Collection, Texas Tech University, Lubbock, Texas; Alfredo Albidrez, Jr. to Yolanda Romero, January 11, 1987, Oral History, Southwest Collection, Texas Tech University, Lubbock, Texas.

SOUTHERN VIETNAMESE NATIONALISM AS ANALOGOUS TO A NURSE LOG

Roy Vũ

Nurse Log Analogy in Human Nature

"Tall, wide trees in the forests of the Pacific Northwest serve as nurse logs to their seedlings after they fall, providing decades of water and nutrients as they slowly decay."

—SIR DAVID ATTENBOROUGH[1]

Analogous to a nurse log—a fallen tree that provides some of the essential ingredients for seedlings to grow—the former Republic of Việt Nam[2] (often referred to as South Việt Nam) provided some of the necessary growing medium for new Vietnamese Americans, imparting knowledge and an identity as their lives began to take root in the United States, which then grows the reorientation of the re-imagined homeland that is more sustainable for the Vietnamese diaspora.

In their post-war resettlement in the United States, Vietnamese Americans have found a new home—once perceived as temporary, but now, for most, permanent. Yet, memories never truly die. What is practiced by generation after generation becomes habitual, part of the culture—even when your homeland is now a ghost land. For Vietnamese Americans, the common cultural praxis not only includes an anticommunist narrative, but also comprises memories from the war, as well as from before and after the war. With these memories, fragments of their homeland connected and jarred together, they discover and recreate both a sanctuary—from the traumas of war, exile, and acculturation—and a new homeland.

Birth of a Post-Apocalyptic Diaspora

In his poignant study on the Army of the Republic of Việt Nam (ARVN), better known as the South Vietnamese Army, *Life and Death in the South Vietnamese Army*, Robert Brigham asserts: "The war against the Communists became a sideshow for many ARVN troops because they were all too aware of their government's own shortcomings."[3] In addition, "The troops fought to survive as members of extended families but not as members of a nation with rich memories of past sacrifices made together or a commitment to present-day common life."[4] Furthermore, Brigham argues that Southern Vietnamese nationalism was a reactionary sentiment to the advancing popularity of communism, and therefore, the ARVN soldiers were fully aware that their government, the RVN, did not have much legitimacy or moral authority since it neither provided nor pinpointed an ideological or political cause—a nationalist legitimacy to which the soldiers could claim they were fighting for or that they could believe in.

However, ARVN soldiers knew what they were fighting *against* but they felt much more ambivalent about what they were fighting *for*, particularly since the RVN government ultimately proved to be too corrupt, disorganized, and inept to rally the troops and its citizens to stand and fight for a legitimate cause, a cause that RVN's administration could not produce on its own. The awareness of what Vietnamese anticommunists were fighting against and the ambivalence of what they were defending and fighting for remain substantially impactful in the Vietnamese diaspora today.

The Communists' complete victory over Southern Việt Nam[5] led to a massive exodus of Vietnamese refugees who braved the seas, seeking a host country where they could at least temporarily stay as political refugees. With the Communist takeover of Southern Việt Nam on April 30, 1975, approximately 130,000 Vietnamese refugees fled Việt Nam and resettled in several host nations, including the United States. In the United States, four temporary refugee reception centers were established to help resettle thousands of Vietnamese refugees: Camp Pendleton, California; Fort Chaffee, Arkansas; Fort Indiantown Gap, Pennsylvania; and Eglin Air Force Base, Florida.

For Vietnamese refugees in America, particularly those who were detained in re-education camps, the United States as a homeland, no matter how grateful they are to the host nation, would be secondary to the Republic of Việt Nam as the primary homeland. Nguyễn Văn Yên[6] writes, "Again and again, all the ARVN officers living in the United States are always willing to adapt themselves to the normal life in this country in order that they and their children can improve their lives, and in the future, can contribute something, even little, according to their capability, to the second homeland—the United States of America."[7] Yet, the passing of time in regard to the memory of war, and the dawning of a post-Cold War reality, would alter the Vietnamese American diaspora's perception of the United States as not just a host country but as a homeland as well.

Despite their struggles with refuge, resettlement, and racialization, Vietnamese Americans' reorientation of Southern Vietnamese history, via the advocacy and promotion of the anticommunist narrative, aligns with the U.S. imperial and Cold War ideologies. By reconceptualizing the history and retaining the memory of Southern Việt Nam, Vietnamese Americans established transhistorical spaces and boundaries with ethnic enclaves—some dubbed Little Saigon (Sài Gòn)—memorials honoring RVN soldiers and refugees, and "Communist-free" zones. However, alternative narratives arise, forged by the American-raised and -born generations of the Vietnamese diaspora, who seek and explore new paths to construct a more complete history. Akin to a nurse log, a fallen, decomposing tree that has provided life to new plants and trees rooted and grown from it, Southern Vietnamese nationalism continues to nurture the Vietnamese diaspora, even though Southern Việt Nam has been gone for more than 40 years.

Racialization of the Vietnamese: The Vietnamese as the Marginalized "Other"

Not all Americans welcomed Vietnamese refugees into the country during the mid-1970s.[8] Nhi Liễu declares: "Consequently, the mass exodus out of Vietnam consisted of a heterogeneous and diverse population of Vietnamese who suddenly became homogenized as 'refugees.'"[9] Americans further expressed their anti-refugee sentiment in a Gallup Poll taken in May of 1975 indicating that 54 percent of all Americans were opposed to admitting Vietnamese refugees to live in the United States while only 36 percent were in favor. Liễu adds: "With a depressed state of the economy, historical amnesia, and xenophobia, nativist sentiment was not only common but unsurprising given the history of U.S. immigration policy, particularly toward Asian immigrants throughout the late nineteenth and most of the twentieth centuries. Moreover, resistance against the refugees also reveals that the nation remained unresolved, unhealed, and divided over its involvement in Vietnam."[10] Despite national reaction against the refugees, with President Gerald Ford's urging, the U.S. government eagerly came to the aid of the people they were unable to assist in winning a long, drawn-out war because they were convinced that it was now their responsibility to aid these displaced émigrés. Liễu argues: "The strategies policymakers used to mobilize public sentiment and justify legislation simultaneously placed Vietnamese refugees in a conservative Cold War political discourse of anticommunism and excluded them from the contemporaneous intense discourse of race and civil rights in U.S. society."[11]

In Houston, some local groups and politicians worried openly about the economic impact of these new refugees on jobs, welfare, and government services; some deployed racist tropes of contagion and cited the refugees bringing in tropical diseases.[12] With the influx of Vietnamese refugees after 1978, a nationwide Harris Poll found that 62 to 72 percent of the respondents believed that there were numerous problems resettling the Vietnamese refugees right after the war, and thus, it would be a mistake to allow more to settle in the United States.[13] The differences in customs and appearance, combined with the Vietnamese emphasis on industriousness and lack of observance of local mores and laws, such as overharvesting of shrimp, also caused tensions in housing and employment.[14]

Conflicts arose as Texan shrimpers accused the Vietnamese fishermen along Texas' Gulf Coast of overharvesting shrimp.[15] The Vietnamese shrimpers were surprised that their hard work would incur resentment and anger among many native Texans. Native Texans along the Gulf Coast exhibited a sense of entitlement that stemmed from the fact that many not only were born and raised in the area, but also inherited the same occupations and were accustomed to their fishing and shrimping lifestyle. Therefore, the Vietnamese "latecomers" were perceived as an invading force, who disrupted their work space and home community.

Reconstructing Southern Việt Nam via Little Sài Gòns and Vietnamese Enclaves

After the turbulent times of refuge, resettlement, and racialization, Vietnamese refugees came to the somber realization that their stay in the United States would be permanent. Critical factors in the process of community formation were (1) to redeem transhistorical Southern Vietnamese nationalism by galvanizing political capital[16] through strident, anticommunist activism *and* changing the anticommunist narrative, and (2) to create platiality[17] that engendered feelings of belonging through establishment of smaller social communities, major shifts in central business districts (CBDs), and the establishment of religious, linguistic, and social service institutions.

Eventually, thousands of Vietnamese refugees made a secondary migration after their initial place of resettlement. Liễu states: "Southern California became a popular destination for secondary migration, and Orange County provided an ideal environment for the new immigrants for numerous reasons."[18] According to Liễu, Southern California in the 1970s offered relatively affordable housing and cheap real estate.[19] In addition, Vietnamese refugees resettled in Southern California in large numbers due to the area's hospitable climate and many job opportunities in the nearby technology and defense industries that were set up during the height of the Cold War. Furthermore, Orange County was desirable because of its close proximity to Camp Pendleton, one of the aforementioned Vietnamese refugee camps opened in 1975 during U.S. Operation New Life. Liễu reasons: "The refugees chose to remain close to Camp Pendleton so that they could be reunited with other family members from whom they had been separated during the process of evacuation."[20]

Linda Võ accurately declares: "Little Saigon in Orange County, California is considered the capital of Vietnamese America and officially encompasses three cities: Westminster, Garden Grove, and Santa Ana. These once sedate suburban communities, about forty-five miles south of Los Angeles, were facing economic decline with their dilapidated structures, but are now marked by thousands of thriving Vietnamese businesses, which provide commercial goods and professional services."[21] With the immediate growth, development, and relative prosperity of Little Sài Gòn in Orange

County, California, formal recognition from city officials would come to designate the Vietnamese ethnic enclave and business district. Liễu asserts: "When Little Saigon finally received official name recognition and designation as a tourist zone, these formalities renewed the spirits of the refugees and marked a great revival of the lost nation."[22] She further argues: "Perhaps more than fulfilling commercial and consumerist desires, it has become a place that nurtures political, social, cultural, and emotional needs—essentially, a place that replaced the lost nation."[23]

Red Scare: Transnational Violence in Little Sài Gòns

For Vietnamese Americans, condemning communism became a temporary useful political tool to not only unify the community, but also convey a shared sense of loss and anger toward the Vietnamese Communist government that has taken away their homeland and persecuted their Southern Vietnamese brethren after the war. Liễu argues: "The double position of being racialized minority subjects and refugees escaping from a repressive communist regime allowed the Vietnamese to articulate a politics that would benefit their vision of American acceptance."[24] As a result, remembering and honoring their homeland of Southern Việt Nam and collaborating with the U.S. government, a hegemonic ally during the Việt Nam War, to denounce the human rights violations committed by the Communist regime are powerful political strategies that further community formation.

In her masterful work, *Transnationalizing Việt Nam: Community, Culture, and Politics in the Diaspora*, Kiều-Linh Caroline Valverde declares: "Dozens of organizations have arisen for the sole purpose of advancing anticommunist ideology and have come to dominate overseas Vietnamese communities. Expressions of anticommunist sentiments from these groups and individuals have resulted in assassinations, protests, and social exclusion."[25] She further observes: "Fear of not adhering to anticommunist dogma, in particular, has placed most Vietnamese Americans in a Foucauldian state of self-monitoring. The ethnic enclave essentially serves as a prison and the rabid anticommunists as its guards. Because of the consequences of straying from the dominant ideology, the disciplined individual practices self-control even without the physical presence of guards."[26]

Founded on June 30, 1981, by former Southern Vietnamese military officers in California, the National United Front for the Liberation of Việt Nam (*Mặt Trận Quốc Gia Thống Nhất Giải Phóng Việt Nam*), or simply the Front, offered refugees a plan to retake their homeland.[27] The scheme to raise a guerrilla army in the countries bordering Việt Nam sounded far-fetched, but was nonetheless enticing. Strong anticommunist sentiment gained momentum in the late 1970s and early 1980s as the Front garnered popular support not just in Little Sài Gòns in Orange County and San Jose, California, but also in Houston, Texas. The group had considerable financial backing and the donors believed they were aiding a good cause—to assist the Front's guerrilla war in Southeast Asia and throttle the Vietnamese Communists.

In Houston, one Vietnamese journalist dared to challenge the Front's political motives and funding activities and thus questioned the community's political agency of anticommunist politics. Nguyễn Đam Phong left Sài Gòn in 1975 and started a newspaper in Houston called *Tự Do*, meaning "freedom."[28] Nguyễn exposed fraudulent refugee aid programs and reported other groups as dishonest.[29] Although he was a fierce anticommunist, Nguyen dedicated his final issues of *Tự Do* to a series accusing the Front's leaders of fraud. Nguyen's paper received anonymous phone threats, fellow journalists pleaded with him to back off, and Nguyen even started carrying a gun. On the early morning of August 25, 1982, he was murdered on the doorstep of his house in southeast Houston.[30] The crime remains unsolved. Vietnamese American community leaders and the Houston Police Department (HPD) suspected that his assassination was the direct result of the articles he published about the Front. The HPD report pointed to the anticommunist organization as the main suspect. The FBI eventually indicted leaders of the Front for money laundering, extortion, bribery, and misappropriation of funds when members used generous donations from the Vietnamese community to run their own restaurant chain and produce adult films. Along with these scandals and the death of the group's leader, Admiral Hoàng Cơ Minh (whose failed attempt to raise an anticommunist guerrilla army in Southeast Asia ended with his death), disenchantment with the Front led to its decline by the early 1990s.

With the demise of the Front by the late 1980s and the Government of Free Việt Nam (GFVN)—another virulent anticommunist organization that originated in southern California—by the late 1990s, more Vietnamese Americans turned to a new post-war narrative that is less virulent yet still decidedly anticommunist. Moving gradually away from redemption and toward reorientation of Southern Vietnamese nationalism, recent changes in the anticommunist narrative, which focus on community formation strategies and platiality, have become a more sustainable alternative for the Vietnamese diaspora. The dissipation of the Front and the decline of the GFVN paved the way for Vietnamese to seek alternative political strategies by the start of the community's third decade, ongoing red-baiting practices notwithstanding.

However, Liễu argues: "Anticommunist politics have functioned as a distinct marker of cultural identity for the Vietnamese diaspora. The public and often most vocal desire to steadfastly embrace anticommunist sentiments has heightened, especially during a time when commodities, people, and cultural forms cross borders and defy territorialization."[31] She concludes: "The American Dream for Vietnamese refugees and immigrants was generated and powered by nostalgia and a stake in both the sameness and the repetition of nostalgic experiences as well as the novelty of a cultural identity invested in consumption and commodity capitalism."[32]

Reorientation of Southern Vietnamese Nationalism

Despite the fact that the RVN is a "dead" country that ceased to exist in 1975, any preconceived notion of a successful overthrow of the Vietnamese Communist Party and the creation of a "democratic" Việt Nam would prove to be far-fetched since the attempt to reconstruct a "pre-1975" RVN nation-state may be quixotic. Linda Võ's argument that we could never truly return home is certainly true in this regard: recreating a pre-1975 RVN is not what Vietnamese people today in Việt Nam would desire to construct; it is merely an imagined homeland fantasy concocted by the anticommunist Vietnamese diaspora. I would further add: There (Southern Việt Nam) neither exists over there (Việt Nam), nor it may not exist much longer over here (Vietnamese diasporic communities), as it is being reoriented as a Vietnamese American re-imagination. Therefore, transhistoricalism may be an appropriate examination of the Vietnamese diaspora's attempt to reorient this re-imagined homeland fantasy in the United States and abroad to further sustain the overseas Vietnamese population.

An increasing number of Vietnamese Americans are more receptive toward conducting transnational linkages, such as continued financial remittances to Việt Nam, returning to their native land, and even acknowledging U.S. cooperation with Việt Nam as inevitable progress for the two nations to heal the old wounds of war. Nevertheless, performing transhistorical Southern Vietnamese nationalism continues to be strong and ubiquitous within Little Sài Gòns as RVN flags are hoisted above restaurants, residential complexes, and stores where Vietnamese Americans congregate, socialize, shop, dine, and conduct their businesses.

Yet, Vietnamese Americans are not necessarily stuck in the quagmire of anticommunist politics. For instance, the Vietnamese American community in Houston erected a Việt Nam War memorial at a shopping center parking lot, at 11360 Bellaire Boulevard, featuring statues of American and Vietnamese soldiers, readying for combat side by side.[33] The statues stand atop of a base, which includes the following inscription:

> To the eternal memory of
>
> the freedom loving people of South Vietnam,
>
> our valiant servicemen, political cadres and civilian employees
>
> who fought relentlessly against the communist aggressors,
>
> and our courageous American comrades-in-arms who sacrificed
>
> themselves for freedom and democracy.
>
> Houston, TX, USA
>
> June 11th, 2005[34]

The base of the statue also includes a dedication to the 1954 Vietnamese refugees who took the opportunity to migrate from the communist north to Southern Việt Nam, after the Geneva Accords set a temporary partition of Việt Nam.[35] Adjacent to this memorial in the same shopping center parking lot, stands another memorial—this one dedicated to refugees—depicting statues of what appears to be a family of Vietnamese refugees from 1975. This memorial holds particular interest for two reasons: (1) It appears to fit into the anticommunist narrative and the "victim" role often projected onto refugees and diaspora populaces; and (2) a post-anticommunist narrative of reorienting the past is visibly present as the refugees' eyes are gazing upward and forward to perhaps an alternative future from the traumas of war, refuge, and resettlement. Thus, the Việt Nam War refugee memorial appears to project a new transhistorical path, one that diverges from the Việt Nam War memorial in Westminster, California, where Southern Vietnamese nationalism appears more prominent and conspicuous.

Memorial in dedication to RVN and U.S. soldiers, located at the Universal Shopping Center parking lot on Bellaire Boulevard in southwest Houston. The memorial was sculpted by Vũ Văn Nhật. (*Photo taken by Roy Vũ, August 27, 2005.*)

Memorial in dedication to Vietnamese refugees, located at the Universal Shopping Center parking lot on Bellaire Boulevard in southwest Houston. The memorial was sculpted by Vũ Văn Nhật. (*Photo taken by Roy Vũ, August 27, 2005.*)

Post-anticommunism Days Ahead?

No doubt, Vietnamese anticommunist politics remains strong and vibrant. Yet simulta-neously, more and more Vietnamese Americans are bucking the old political trends and establishing new ones such as embracing the need to become more involved in the U.S. political system, establishing transnational ties with Việt Nam, and reconstructing their community and place through new anticommunist political strategies. Such transformation allows the Vietnamese to address the social and economic problems here in their commu-nity as well as give diverse opinions on international matters pertaining to Việt Nam.

Meanwhile, remittances from Vietnamese Americans to their family and relatives in Việt Nam continue to increase. The financial amount of family remittances to Việt Nam increased from $1.2 billion in 1999 to $7.2 billion in 2008, and exceeding $8 billion in 2010.[36] Valverde further adds: "Also, humanitarian projects in Việt Nam set up by overseas Vietnamese not only help people in need in the home country but also allow those in diaspora to have direct influence there. To collect funds in the United States, non-profits carefully ensure that helping Vietnamese citizens does not carry hints of propping up the communist regime."[37]

Võ asserts: "As a younger generation comes of age that does not harbor the same animosity towards the Communist regime and with more Vietnamese Americans traveling to Việt Nam to visit relatives, for charity work, and to establish business enterprises, the focus on anti-Communist issues will be less pronounced or not tak-en so seriously."[38] Referencing the political transference theory, Võ further analyzes: "Vietnamese American political involvement in their home country can account for their willingness to engage in the U.S. political system, debunking the myth of new-comers who are apathetic to the political process."[39]

A question then beckons us to ask: Would future generations maintain such an an-ticommunist narrative path or diverge into new or lesser-known interstitial paths that would help them reconcile with the past yet forge on forwardly, even if the myopic twin narratives of the Horatio Alger-like stories of the successful immigrant and the glorified savior–victim refugee stories remain hegemonic in U.S. history psyche? For certain, current attempts to bridge generations via transhistorical reorientation of the past will not suffice if interstitial spaces for other narratives remain unopened or unex-plored. As Liễu attests: "Neither static nor pure, Vietnamese culture has always been in flux—an unstable process that is always in motion."[40]

Conclusion

Similar to a nurse log, Southern Vietnamese nationalism has provided the necessary nutrients for Vietnamese American communities to start, grow, and develop to size-able and influential ethnic business districts and neighborhoods. At times, Southern Vietnamese nationalism has duly served to unify the overseas Vietnamese populace, and its anticommunist narrative has acceptably fitted with the U.S. Cold War ideology. Thus, such a narrative protects Vietnamese Americans from further racialization and marginalization. However, Southern Vietnamese nationalism has also divided the Vietnamese diaspora and stifled more possible growth and development for a resettled population that has not tolerated diverse political opinions nor dissent. In other words, for Vietnamese American communities to sustain themselves, the populace must have an opportunity to differentiate and identify itself anew, not apart, from its source of origin—the nurse log that is Southern Vietnamese nationalism.

Notes

1. http://www.asknature.org/strategy/e0c8517027aa8edf4507a8624425e89f, accessed September 19, 2005. See also David Attenborough, The Private Life of Plants: A Natural History of Plant Behavior (London: BBC Books, 1995), 180.

2. I prefer to use the more traditional spellings of Việt Nam and Sài Gòn. However, when cited or quoted from other sources, their spellings will be used in accordance to their respective authors and common-place public acknowledgment.

3. Robert K. Brigham, ARVN: Life and Death in the South Vietnamese Army (Lawrence: University Press of Kansas, 2006), 121.

4. Ibid.

5. South Việt Nam is sometimes referred to as Southern Việt Nam. Please see Robert Buzzanco, Masters of War: Military Dissent and Politics in the Vietnam Era (Cambridge: Cambridge University Press, 1997). His reference to South Việt Nam as Southern Việt Nam is to provide a clearer purpose behind the establishment of South Việt Nam as a created state mandated by the Geneva Accords and not the will of the Southern Vietnamese populace. Thus, Southern Việt Nam was separated from the rest of Việt Nam, and based on that perspective, there was no such thing as a separate North and South Việt Nam but rather a single country and population that was divided by the geopolitics of the Cold War between the United States and Soviet Union.

6. I prefer to use the traditional spelling and order of Vietnamese names, where the surname is stated first, unless the person's name order is publicly known in accordance with English language standards.

7. Yen Văn Nguyễn, The Destiny of the Soldiers of the Army of the Republic of Việt Nam Living in the United States under Refugee Status, MS-SEA027, Box 1, Folder 14 (Irvine, CA: UC Irvine Libraries Southeast Asian Archives, February 18, 1992), 3.

8. Fred R. Von der Mehden, The Ethnic Groups of Houston (Houston: Rice University Studies, 1984), 88.

9. Nhi T. Liễu, The American Dream in Vietnamese (Minneapolis: University of Minnesota Press, 2011), 8.

10. Ibid., 10.

11. Ibid., 13.

12. Von der Mehden, The Ethnic Groups of Houston, 98.

13. Ibid.

14. Ibid.

15. Communication and Language Line, Inc., Non-Traditional Crime in America: A Handbook for Law Enforcement Officers, Robert Walsh Collection, Box 1, Folder 19 (Irvine, CA: UC Irvine Libraries Special Collections and Archives, April 1989), 12.

16. In this setting, political capital relates to the ability and availability of not only using a community's resources, but also expanding such resources to further a political agenda or cause. For the Vietnamese diaspora, staunch anticommunist community leaders, elected or self-appointed, call for their constituents to pool in their resources and unite for a greater cause, in this case, the continuing struggle against Vietnamese communism.

17. Karin Aguilar-San Juan, Little Saigons: Staying Vietnamese in America (Minneapolis: University of Minnesota Press, 2009), xxvi. Platiality connotes a greater sense of home and belonging for an individual, or place could represent a "living and breathing" community for a group of people who have valued it. Platiality is a place that has meaning to someone or a group of people, more so than space that can be limited to a place that is void of value before platiality or place-making occurs. Platiality differs from

spatiality. Space may have dimensions, but place-making is the use of such dimensions to give the space a value.

18. Liễu, The American Dream in Vietnamese, 32–33.

19. Ibid.

20. Ibid.

21. Linda Trinh Võ, "Constructing a Vietnamese American Community: Economic and Political Transformation in Little Saigon, Orange County," Special issue: "How Do Asian Americans Create Places? Los Angeles and Beyond," Amerasia Journal 34 (3) (2008): 85.

22. Liễu, The American Dream in Vietnamese, 41.

23. Ibid., 57.

24. Ibid., 13.

25. Kiều-Linh Caroline Valverde, Transnationalizing Viet Nam: Community, Culture, and Politics in the Diaspora (Philadelphia: Temple University Press, 2013), 12.

26. Ibid., 111.

27. Claudia Kolker, "Casualties of War," Houston Press, February 9–15, 1995.

28. Jo Ann Zuniga, "Group Calls Editor's Slaying Here Political: Vietnamese Journalist Murdered in '82," Houston Chronicle, December 5, 1994.

29. Kolker, "Casualties of War."

30. Ibid.

31. Liễu, The American Dream in Vietnamese, 130.

32. Ibid., 133.

33. Lindsey Wise, "Veteran Chronicles: Việtnam War Memorials," Houston Chronicle, November 10, 2011.

34. www.waymarking.com, accessed April 19, 2014.

35. "Việtnam Memorial Honors War Veterans, Two Refugee Movements," accessed April 19, 2014, www.youtube.com.

36. Valverde, Transnationalizing Việt Nam, 16.

37. Ibid., 149.

38. Võ, "Constructing a Vietnamese American Community," 99.

39. Ibid., 100.

40. Liễu, The American Dream in Vietnamese, 134.

MARCH OF FAITH
(NOVEMBER 7, 1971)

Yolanda Romero

In 1971, the March of Faith was organized by the Mexican American youth activists of Lubbock, a Brown Beret Chapter, and the elders in the community with the help of the Department of Community Relations. In planning the protest, the March organizers held meetings at the Guadalupe Center in the heart of the *barrio* and emphasized the message to participants that became the motto of the March, "peace and faith." For the sake of the credibility of the Mexican American community, it became vital that no violence occur during or after the March. Leaders urged all participants to ignore any unfriendly remarks or gestures from Anglo onlookers or policemen. The organizers further urged participants to stay away from the March if they had any reservations about controlling their tempers or actions against Anglo agitators. The men in the community, joined by the Brown Berets, volunteered to walk alongside the crowd to act as "lookouts" against any trouble. The Brown Beret Chapter of Lubbock received support to guard the marchers when Father Jaramillo from New Mexico brought the Brown Beret Chapter from that state to help with the March.

At Mose Hood Park on Ave. Q, prior to the March there was a religious ceremony held for the people. On that dreary, misty, and cold fall day, approximately 500 Mexican Americans and their supporters gathered at the park and sang songs before beginning the March. The March began at the park and traveled north on Ave. Q, turning east on Broadway until it reached the Lubbock County Courthouse. The feeling that engulfed the crowd was so overwhelming that many cried and embraced their neighbor. The banner of *La Virgen de Guadalupe* waved at the head of the March, and the people followed, many carrying posters and others raising their clinched fist and shouting at the top of their voices, "Chicano Power!" The crowd grew, as many of the parents, worried about their children, and other onlookers followed the crowd but were overwhelmed by the commitment and the show of pride, and they too joined the March. Many Anglo residents witnessing this display of "Chicano Power" appeared to be amused, while others had a horrified look on their faces as the marchers passed through the streets.

At the courthouse, Mariano Garcia, Chon Garcia, and Joe Rangel acted as spokesmen for the Mexican American community. They submitted to the city 23 grievances and demands compiled by students, businessmen, ministers, priests, laborers, and housewives from the various Lubbock *barrios*. These grievances and demands fell into five categories: justice, equal protection under the law, fair representation, equal employment, and education. Eight months after the March, the Lubbock City Council and Civil Service Commission reacting to one of the demands lowered the height requirements for police officers. The minimum height became 5'7", enabling many young Mexican American men to get jobs as policemen.

References

Gilbert Herrera to Yolanda Romero, Oral Interview, July 2, 1985, at Lubbock, Texas, Southwest Collection, Texas Tech University; Juan Perez to Yolanda Romero, Oral Interview, July 25, 1985, at Lubbock, Texas, Southwest Collection, Texas Tech University; *El Editor*, Lubbock, Texas, October 12, 1977; Lucas Trujillo to Yolanda Romero, Oral Interview, March 24, 1987, at Piano, Texas, Southwest Collection, Texas Tech University; Bidal Aguero Papers, Southwest Collection, Texas Tech University; Nephtali De Leon Papers, Southwest Collection, Texas Tech University; Nephtali De Leon, *Chicanos: Our Background and Our Pride* (Lubbock, TX: Trucha Publications, 1972), pp. 70–74; Andres Tijerina, *Mexican Americans in Lubbock County* (Lubbock, TX: Texas Tech Press, 1979), p. 66; *La Voz de* Texas, Lubbock, Texas, August 11, 1972.

GENERATION MONARCH: PATHWAYS OF MIGRATION IN THE TWENTY-FIRST CENTURY

Brandon Morton

Imagine for a moment, it's late August in Canada, and you are living near the northern shores of the Great Lakes, near Toronto. The days are beginning to get cooler and the nights are beginning to get longer. You are about to leave the place your parents, grandparents, and generations before them built for you. The journey you are about to embark on will take a distance of approximately 3,000 kilometers and you are racing against the seasonal change from fall to winter, to avoid the upcoming freezing winter temperatures and snowfall. You will not have maps, satellites, or technology to help guide you to your destination. In fact, you have never been to your destination. Only your ancestors' ancestors and the great traveling generations of your forefathers have been there. But something inside you tells you the way. Somehow, you can feel which path is the right path. You have what it takes to make it, but there are obstacles in your way the entire journey. These obstacles may threaten your life, family, or friends.

This is not the story of immigration, though it could be. This is the story of the North American monarch butterfly, *Danaus plexippus*, the official state insect of Alabama, Idaho, Illinois, Minnesota, Texas, and West Virginia.

Monarch butterflies can be easily identified by their black and orange and white markings. They are also known for their unique migration behavior and expansive habitat. Monarchs are the only butterflies in the world that migrate similarly to birds. States such as Texas are well known by international birdwatchers and monarch-watchers as important states for habitat protection because of monarch's migratory behavior. Most monarchs live only for a few weeks, but the last generation of the season, born in late August, is the migratory generation and lives for as long as eight months. All other generations dedicate their lives, passing on information to the next generation in order to accomplish the ultimate goal, to make sure the youngest generation would make the journey back to their winter home in Mexico.

One summer home to monarchs is in Canada, just north of the Great Lakes. When the season is about to change from fall to winter, the youngest monarch starts the migratory path to its winter home, 3,000 kilometers south in the oyamel fir trees of the Transvolcanic Mountain Range near Mexico City. At this southernmost point of the monarch migratory pathway, temperatures normally do not reach freezing point, 0°C or 32°F. The multigenerational migration of monarch butterflies is a testament to the connections a population of organisms has with their environment, to distinguish a correct direction from an incorrect direction with an internal compass. The monarch's internal compass is a collaboration of sensory cues and environmental factors such as daylight hours, number of days in a row with the right temperature, and magnetic fields, which serve as navigation signs similar to a man-made compass that points north. However, climate changes alter environmental cues to the monarchs, and as a result alter their range and behavior. Today, the climate seems to be changing faster than before and is thought to be one cause for the decline in butterfly populations.

Monarch population decline has been reported widely by many backyard gardeners, birdwatchers, and scientific researchers. At one point, researchers estimated as many as 1 billion monarchs made North America their home. Today, research with the help of citizen science monitors estimates that only 56 million monarchs remain. Citizen scientists have played a major role in increasing understanding of monarchs and helping to track their populations, plants such as milkweed, and the various life stages of the monarch.

A citizen scientist is a volunteer in a community who contributes her or his time collecting data, and then reporting the data to an organization or a professional scientist. Citizen scientists are involved with many different organizations and collect data for a wide variety of ecological measurements like pollinator populations or environmental measurements like rainfall or water quality. This community-based science collaboration helps create better informed policy decisions for government representatives, business leaders, and other organization leaders. An example program by the University of Minnesota, called *Monarch Larva Monitoring Project*, coordinates over 900 citizen scientists in Canada, Mexico, and the United States to help track the monarch butterfly larvae, commonly referred to as a caterpillar. The monarch butterfly lays over 400 eggs and the young larvae hatch and grow by eating milkweeds. Milkweeds come in various types depending on geographic location, or ecoregion, and are the required food source and habitat for monarchs.

In early 2015, the United States Fish and Wildlife Service (FWS) announced a one-year study to explore the health of the monarch butterflies in North America. The results of this study will determine if the monarchs will be designated on the list according to the Endangered Species Act of 1973. If listed as an endangered species, any and all landowners, both public and private, will be required to take action to improve protection of all monarchs along the migratory pathways of the monarch populations. The FWS launched this study in response to a citizen's coalition and petition to protect the monarchs. The petition included significant scientific evidence from universities, private institutions, and corporations describing potential causes of the monarch butterfly population decline. Potential causes of population decline include:

- Habitat loss from deforestation for agricultural, industrial, and residential growth.
- Bioaccumulation of herbicides such as Roundup™ used by large-scale farms for crops like corn or soy.
- Declining number of milkweed plants due to intensive drought and herbicide use.
- Increasing number of severe storms and droughts compared to previous migration years.

The monarch butterfly could very well be the "canary in the coal mine" of the twenty-first century. The early coal miners brought down a canary bird in a cage as a biological indicator of potential health risks. In a worst-case scenario, if the canary falls ill or dies, then the coal miners have little time to escape the danger of gases and fumes being emitted from deep in the earthen rock that harmed the canary.

The monarch butterfly population decline represents a multigenerational challenge across the entire continent of North America. Monarchs are impacted greatly by human activity, and if communities and organizations do not address the decline of the monarchs, humans may not be able to last for future generations. As part of the ecosystem, people are most connected to their neighborhood community. The way people impact air quality, land quality, and water quality contributes to individual health, relationship health, community health, and societal health. Like the canary in the coal mine, if the monarch butterfly is North America's biological indicator, there needs to be an increased focus on environmental restoration to reverse the degradation of our communities and ecosystems.

The monarch butterfly could also be a symbol of sustainability, in particular, the concept of seven generations. The concept of seven generations comes from several indigenous or Native cultures that have lived so closely with the environment for so long and have passed down oral traditions about the importance and roles of local animals, plants, soil, and water. This passed-down knowledge from generation to generation teaches each generation to care for the community beyond their own great, great, great, great grandchildren. The seventh generation is your yet-to-be-born relatives, family, and friends. The extended family and friends structure beyond the living generations is the most sustainable social system of organization based on collective ownership that supports survival of future generations. From this perspective, it is fundamentally imperative to incorporate historical environmental knowledge into practices and policies for sustainable development.

In the urbanizing modern world, collectively known as the G7 and G20 countries, industrialized countries have passed down from generation to generation a culture of harvesting natural resources with disregard for any capacity limit. However, every ecosystem has a carrying capacity that differs for every organism. Carrying capacity is based on limited resource factors such as food, habitat, and water, and biological fitness—ability of offspring to reproduce.

The modern method of transferring knowledge of individual dreams and community goals has allowed for development of technology and practices to improve our quality of life, and ultimately increase the relative pace of life and geographical range of an individual over a short period of time. This increased pace and range of human activities is having a dramatic impact on the planet, especially for species like the monarch butterfly.

Entomologists and wildlife biologists still do not fully understand how the monarchs communicate from generation to generation, to ensure the health of the last generation of the season that will make the 3,000-kilometer journey home and back again. There are important parallels to learn from the monarch, even if we do not fully understand them. The actions people can take can impact generations. Like the monarch, it is imperative to humanity's survival that we transfer the best practices and planetary knowledge beyond the seventh generation. Also, in 2015, President Barack Obama announced a National Strategy to Promote Health of Honey Bees and Other Pollinators. In this strategy, he calls for a transcontinental corridor to protect the monarch butterfly migratory pathway. With the help of all ages of citizen scientists, this new strategy will help increase populations of pollinators like honey bees and monarchs. Our agricultural food system and way of life depend on it.

A DOUBLE HOME LOSS? THE INVISIBLE SPACE OF LITTLE SÀI GÒN IN MIDTOWN HOUSTON

Roy Vũ

Introduction

As a history graduate student from the University of Houston, I took notice of the gradual deterioration of the Little Sài Gòn commercial district in the Midtown area adjacent to downtown Houston. In the summer of 2005, I decided to venture out to Little Sài Gòn to take some photos of what remained of the once-thriving Vietnamese central business district. Sifting through the photos, I cannot help but lament and feel nostalgic for the old Little Sài Gòn to remain as it was before the district went into decline. Nonetheless, perhaps for my own personal edification, I am glad that I took pictures of what was left of Little Sài Gòn before it completely disappears physically and from memory. Perhaps in a small way, the selected photos for this essay will preserve Little Sài Gòn and prevent its complete erasure from history.

For Vietnamese Houstonians, the waning of Little Sài Gòn and its inevitable end signify a double home loss. When Southern Việt Nam (often referred to as South Việt Nam or Republic of Việt Nam) was first created as a temporary nation-state by the 1954 Geneva Accords, it was the beginning of an arguably fictitious homeland yet a real one for Vietnamese anticommunists, constructed in the early Cold Wars of the geopolitical struggle between the United States and Soviet Union. With the Communist takeover of Southern Việt Nam and the end of the Việt Nam War (sometimes referred to as the American War or Second Indochina War) on April 30, 1975, approximately 130,000 Vietnamese refugees fled Việt Nam and resettled in several host nations, including the United States. In the United States, four temporary refugee reception centers were established to help resettle thousands of Vietnamese refugees: Camp Pendleton, California; Fort Chaffee, Arkansas; Fort Indiantown Gap, Pennsylvania; and Eglin Air Force Base, Florida. Eventually, thousands of Vietnamese refugees made a secondary migration after their initial place of resettlement. Most Vietnamese refugees resided in California, but many resettled in Houston, Texas, and constructed a multinodal residential and commercial Vietnamese American community. Starting in the mid-1980s, Vietnamese Houstonians established a vibrant, thriving business district dubbed Little Sài Gòn. Unfortunately, toward the end of the 1990s, the Little Sài Gòn commercial district began to decline due to gentrification, rising cost of rent for tenants, a decrease in the number of consumers, and city leaders' attempt to "revitalize" the Midtown district. Consequently, Vietnamese Houstonians are experiencing a double home loss[1]— first, with the suffering from the loss of Southern Việt Nam, and second, gradually losing Little Sài Gòn, a once-vibrant commercial district. Thus, the Vietnamese central business district began to shift once more, and at the start of the twenty-first century, a plethora of Vietnamese-owned businesses were already flourishing along Bellaire Boulevard, transforming the southwest Houston neighborhood into the *de facto* Little Sài Gòn for Vietnamese Houstonians.

Vietnamese Platiality in Houston

The Vietnamese in Houston made a concerted effort to re-establish their homeland in the United States and create a community. As stated in another essay, critical factors in the process of community formation were (1) to redeem transhistorical Southern Vietnamese nationalism[2] by galvanizing political capital[3] through strident, anticommunist activism *and* changing the anticommunist narrative, and (2) to create platiality[4] or "place-making" that engendered feelings of belonging through establishment of smaller social communities, major shifts in central business districts (CBDs), and the establishment of religious, linguistic, and social service institutions.

To construct, preserve, and strengthen their community, Vietnamese Houstonians relied heavily on the anticommunist narrative. They made efforts to redeem the Republic of Việt Nam (RVN) or Southern Vietnamese nationalism to galvanize the community, using political rhetoric and action to denounce communism in hopes of one day returning to a democratic Việt Nam. Upon resettling in Houston, Vietnamese refugees turned to redeeming Southern Vietnamese nationalism, a transhistorical anticommunist narrative from the Cold War to help them establish their platiality, and at times, it overwhelmingly consumed their place-making efforts much to the detriment of the community, particularly during the early resettlement years. In regard to transhistoricalism, it is in reference to the Vietnamese diasporic community's post–Việt Nam War struggle to retain and redeem Southern Vietnamese nationalism despite the fact that the created state of the Republic of Việt Nam ceased to exist in 1975. Transnationalism indicates meaningful linkages between communities from two different, *existing* nations. Transhistoricalism reflects a meaningful and relevant connection of an idea—in this case, Southern Vietnamese nationalism—across time. For the Vietnamese diaspora community, particularly in Houston, Southern Vietnamese nationalism is perceived as a real and tangible idea that remains an integral part of how they live and consume their platiality on a daily basis even though the Republic of Việt Nam has ceased to exist.

Vietnamese Houstonians utilized transhistorical Southern Vietnamese nationalism to help construct their platiality. In the aftermath of the Việt Nam War and resettlement in the United States, Vietnamese in Houston established platiality or place-making, creating a place that remains in flux and constant change as multiple nodes of center coexist—residential neighborhoods and business districts—throughout Houston. Here, "center" is being loosely applied because of the urban sprawl and boundary of Houston itself (due to no formal zoning codes) provides the concurrent existence of multiple nodes of center. Over time, Vietnamese Houstonians forged multiple business districts, three residential areas with a significant Vietnamese population, and several smaller, defined social communities.

Karin Aguilar-San Juan's concept of platiality provides a framework for understanding the Vietnamese community in Houston. In her work, she demonstrates the importance of platiality for the Vietnamese communities in Boston, Massachusetts, and Orange County, California. Platiality emphasizes the act of making place rather than simply inhabiting space.[5] As for the Vietnamese in Houston, they have established and transformed a "place" of their own. Unlike other Vietnamese communities across the United States, Vietnamese Houstonians reside in several major residential areas as well as smaller, defined social communities throughout the city. Furthermore, through the course of the community's history, the Vietnamese commercial district has shifted from one area of Houston to another.

A Brief History of Vietnamese Central Business Districts in Houston

In their early development of commercial platiality, Vietnamese entrepreneurs saved money, pooled their capital, and opened up new businesses next to the old Chinatown since Chinese storeowners would have the Asian clientele Vietnamese business owners desired to attract. In terms of mutual aid networking, many Vietnamese Americans who decided to venture into the discount nail salon industry became successful entrepreneurs. Sociologist Thao Ha explains that Vietnamese American women and men who started their nail salons were able to help friends and family members by giving them advice on the business, showing them techniques, and giving them their first jobs as nail salon technicians.[6] Once they started as nail technicians, they could save enough money to open their own shops. Such strategies helped Vietnamese entrepreneurs survive, succeed, and sustain their business community. Within five years after the fall of Sài Gòn, Vietnamese business districts began to take shape.[7] The Vietnamese businesses quickly developed, not only reviving old business districts of lower rent that preceded their arrival but also expanding other once-decrepit economic sectors. Thus, the discount nail salon industry became a viable economic niche for Vietnamese entrepreneurs, and nail salon-related businesses remained integral to the community's commercial platiality.

The first Vietnamese business district was known as Vinatown, which was established in downtown, nearby Old Chinatown and what is now the George R. Brown Convention Center. However, by the mid-1980s, Vietnamese entrepreneurs began relocating their businesses down the street and farther west along Milam Street.[8] By decade's end, a new "Little Sài Gòn" along the Milam corridor became the key cultural center for Vietnamese Americans to shop, eat, browse, and socialize.[9] Local Vietnamese American leaders under the direction of Nguyễn Cao My,[10] President of the Vietnamese Community of Houston and Vicinities (VNCH) from 1998 to 2002, the community's official liaison group, even passed a resolution to post Vietnamese street signs along Milam Street.[11] By the early 1990s, many Vietnamese-owned businesses were propping up along Milam Street between McGowen and Holman Streets. In recognition of the vibrant number of Vietnamese-owned businesses along the Milam corridor that had revitalized the neighborhood, in 1998 the Houston City Council approved of Vietnamese street signs to be put up in the Midtown District. By May 2004, the area was officially designated as Little Sài Gòn by the city council as it had become the Vietnamese social, cultural, and commercial hub, albeit the commercial district had started to decline by the time it gained formal recognition. Bellaire Boulevard in southwest Houston had already surpassed Little Sài Gòn to become the largest Vietnamese business district. Meanwhile, the official Little Sài Gòn along the Milam corridor continued to wane as a major Vietnamese business district, whereas along Bellaire Boulevard in southwest Houston, Vietnamese-owned businesses continued to thrive, and thus, locals began to refer this area as the new Little Sài Gòn. Bellaire Boulevard has become the true "center" of the Vietnamese community.

A Double Home Loss?

Due to gentrification of the Midtown neighborhood and the rising cost of rent, Houston's Little Sài Gòn community began to collapse. Vietnamese-owned shopping centers, such as the Hoa Binh Center and Phuoc Loe Tho Center, fell into disarray as storefront tenants were confronted with rising expenses and fewer consumers. More and more Vietnamese-owned businesses began to close shop or relocate to the burgeoning and more lucrative business district along Bellaire Boulevard in southwest Houston. One by one, Vietnamese-owned restaurants, bookstores, bakeries, and discount nail salons disappeared in Midtown. In their places were new condominiums and apartments designed to attract young, upper-middle-class professionals looking to reside in an urban setting. To develop such an urban environment, new trendy restaurants, nightclubs, and cafes opened for business along the Milam corridor.

Nevertheless, Vietnamese Houstonians remain resilient and adamant in their attempts to reconstruct a viable homeland away from home. For instance, in the early 1990s, Vietnamese-owned businesses began to prop up and multiply along Bellaire Boulevard in southwest Houston. With the rapid development and proliferation of Vietnamese-owned restaurants, banking institutions, cafes, discount nail salons, and non-profit organizations along Bellaire Boulevard, this commercial district has become the *de facto* Little Sài Gòn of Houston. Hence, in a sense, Little Sài Gòn lives on in Houston but in a different area of the city. However, one would be amiss to disregard the significance of the original Little Sài Gòn and its intangible impact upon Vietnamese Houstonians, a population whose lives and history are in perpetual exile. Vietnamese Americans in Houston suffer from a double home loss since Southern Việt Nam could never be reconstructed in its original nation-state, and second, Little Sài Gòn could never exactly be duplicated. As Houston's original Little Sài Gòn gradually disappeared, particularly with Vietnamese street signs being removed from the Midtown neighborhood, one could sense the significant loss for Vietnamese Houstonians as a part of their resettlement history has been erased due to recent gentrification. Consequently, when revitalization efforts occur in marginalized residential neighborhoods and commercial districts, we must always consider and weigh the intangible costs of gentrification, particularly for those who work and live in places threatened to become gentrified.

Conclusion

After nearly 40 years of resettlement, Vietnamese Americans have established platiality by developing an emerging and vibrant post-war community in Houston through reformulating nationalism and political participation, which in turn helped create small, well-defined social communities, shifting their central business districts, and establishing religious, linguistic, and social service institutions.

Despite enduring the inevitable loss of Midtown's Little Sài Gòn, Vietnamese Houstonians have constructed an exceptional, multinodal community that remains in flux, responding to the constant changes and challenges faced by the community. Perhaps, learning from the steady disappearance of Midtown's Little Sài Gòn, Vietnamese Houstonians are more inclined and equipped with sufficient political capital to further construct and preserve their *de facto* Little Sài Gòn along Bellaire Boulevard. Henceforth, an ethnic community will be sustained, and a part of their history will be preserved, averting a complete double home loss.

U.S. and RVN flags. RVN flags once dominated the Milam corridor. With the gentrification of the Midtown District and subsequent closure of many Vietnamese-owned businesses, RVN flags are no longer omnipresent in the neighborhood. Little Sài Gòn, Midtown District, Houston, TX. (*Photo taken by Roy Vũ, August 24, 2005.*)

Vietnamtown Shopping Center, which no longer exists. Little Sài Gòn, Midtown District, Houston, TX. (*Photo taken by Roy Vũ, August 24, 2005.*)

The adjacent parking lot to the Vietnamtown Shopping Center and its wall of the RVN flag have been removed. Little Sài Gòn, Midtown District, Houston, TX. (*Photo taken by Roy Vũ, August 24, 2005.*)

Vietnamese street signs were once prevalent in Midtown. Now, all Vietnamese street signs have been removed. Little Sài Gòn, Midtown District, Houston, TX. (*Photo taken by Roy Vũ, August 24, 2005.*)

Hoa Binh Shopping Center. Little Sài Gòn, Midtown District, Houston, TX. (*Photo taken by Roy Vũ, August 24, 2005.*)

Hoa Binh Shopping Center, which no longer exists. Little Sài Gòn, Midtown District, Houston, TX. (*Photo taken by Roy Vũ, August 24, 2005.*)

These Vietnamese-owned businesses no longer exist. Little Sài Gòn, Midtown District, Houston, TX. (*Photo taken by Roy Vũ, August 24, 2005.*)

Phuoc Loc Tho Shopping Center, which no longer exists. Little Sài Gòn, Midtown District, Houston, TX. (*Photo taken by Roy Vũ, August 24, 2005.*)

Camden Travis Street Condominiums, one of several recent condominiums constructed along the Milam corridor. Midtown District, Houston, TX. (*Photo taken by Ngọc Vũ, June 25, 2015.*)

A new condominium along Louisiana Street, which runs parallel next to Milam Street. Midtown District, Houston, TX. (*Photo taken by Ngọc Vũ, June 25, 2015.*)

Another new condominium along Louisiana Street. Midtown District, Houston, TX. (*Photo taken by Ngọc Vũ, June 25, 2015.*)

New construction for another condominium is built along Milam Street. Midtown District, Houston, TX. (*Photo taken by Ngọc Vũ, June 25, 2015.*)

Vietnamese street signs, once ubiquitous throughout Midtown, have been removed. Midtown District, Houston, TX. (*Photo taken by Ngọc Vũ, June 25, 2015.*)

A few Vietnamese-owned businesses, such as Les Givral's Sandwich and Cafe, still remain despite gentrification. Midtown District, Houston, TX. (*Photo taken by Ngọc Vũ, June 25, 2015.*)

Bích Nga Hair and Skin Care, one of just a few Vietnamese-owned businesses remaining along Milam Street. Midtown District, Houston, TX. (*Photo taken by Ngọc Vũ, June 25, 2015.*)

Mai's Restaurant, which is still a popular restaurant on Milam Street. After a fire destroyed the building on February 15, 2010, the Vietnamese-owned restaurant was reconstructed and remodeled to match the new architectural landscape brought forth by the gentrification of the neighborhood. Midtown District, Houston, TX. (*Photo taken by Ngọc Vũ, June 25, 2015.*)

Notes

1. If we are to consider the Republic of Việt Nam (Southern Việt Nam), better known as South Việt Nam, to be a fictitious nation-state that artificially existed beyond the 1954 Geneva Accords agreement, then one may argue that the exiled Southern Vietnamese have suffered an imagined double home loss: (1) the imaginary Republic of Việt Nam and (2) the Little Sài Gòn business community in the Midtown District constructed to re-imagine the artificially created Republic of Việt Nam. Hence, one can never go back to the Republic of Việt Nam since there is no "there" left, and therefore, this act by the Vietnamese diaspora to construct a Little Sài Gòn, only to lose it later, may be considered an imaginary double home loss. Nevertheless, the loss remains a real loss for Vietnamese Houstonians. Despite this imaginary double home loss, Vietnamese Houstonians have established a new (unofficial) Little Sài Gòn along Bellaire Boulevard in southwest Houston. Also, a few Vietnamese-owned businesses still remain on Milam Street of the old Little Sài Gòn despite the gentrification of the Midtown neighborhood. Both cases provide evidence of the resilience and hard work put forth by Vietnamese entrepreneurs and the community to create and recreate their own platiality.

2. South Việt Nam is sometimes referred to as Southern Việt Nam. Please see Robert Buzzanco, *Masters of War: Military Dissent and Politics in the Vietnam Era* (Cambridge: Cambridge University Press, 1997). His reference to South Việt Nam as Southern Việt Nam is to provide a clearer purpose behind the establishment of South Việt Nam as a created state mandated by the Geneva Accords and not the will of the Southern Vietnamese populace. Thus, Southern Việt Nam was separated from the rest of Việt Nam, and based on that perspective, there was no such thing as a separate North and South Việt Nam but rather a single country and population that was divided by the geopolitics of the Cold War between the United States and Soviet Union.

3. In this setting, political capital relates to the ability and availability of not only using a community's resources, but also expanding such resources to further a political agenda or cause. For

Vietnamese Americans in Houston and vicinity, staunch anticommunist community leaders, elected or self-appointed, call for their constituents to pool in their resources and unite for a greater cause, in this case, the continuing struggle against Vietnamese communism.

4. Karin Aguilar-San Juan, *Little Saigons: Staying Vietnamese in America* (Minneapolis: University of Minnesota Press, 2009), xxvi.

5. Ibid. Platiality connotes a greater sense of home and belonging for an individual, or place could represent a "living and breathing" community for a group of people who have valued it. Platiality is a place that has *meaning* to someone or a group of people, more so than space that can be limited to a place that is void of value before platiality or place-making occurs. Platiality differs from spatiality. Space may have dimensions, but place-making is the use of such dimensions to give the space a value.

6. Thao Ha, *Ethnic Entrepreneurship: The Case of the Vietnamese Nail Salon* (Houston: University of Houston Thesis Publications, 2003), 10.

7. Ibid.

8. Deborah Jensen, "Houston's Indo-Chinatown: The First Generation," *Cite Magazine*, Winter edition, 1987.

9. Ibid.

10. I prefer to use the traditional spelling and order of Vietnamese names, where the surname is stated first, unless the person's name order is publicly known in accordance with English language standards.

11. Every two years, the Vietnamese Community of Houston and Vicinities (VNCH) would hold an election for new officers. Despite little financial resources and lack of a complete mandate, VNCH is recognized as the unofficial, definitive political voice of Houston's Vietnamese community.

"*ADELANTE COMPAÑEROS*: THE SANITATION WORKERS STRUGGLE IN LUBBOCK, TEXAS, 1968–1972"

Yolanda Romero

The Sanitation Worker's Struggle in Lubbock, Texas, 1968–1972

The 1960s turned into a decade of active involvement in the areas of politics and labor organization for the Mexican American population in Texas. As early as 1960 Mexican Americans were actively organizing "Viva Kennedy" Clubs throughout Texas. In Northwest Texas such clubs could be found in approximately fourteen towns, among them Lubbock, Lamesa, Amarillo, Muleshoe, Brownfield, Plainview, and Hereford.

Reprinted from *Texas Labor History* by Bruce Glassrud and James C. Maroney, Editors and Yolanda G. Romero, Author by permission of The Texas A&M University Press. Copyright © by Texas A&M University Press.

Union organizers recognized the political power Mexican Americans in Texas were gaining and sought to mobilize these voters. Indeed, Mexican Americans won control of the city council in Crystal City in 1963 with the support of the Teamsters Union as well as the Political Association of Spanish-Speaking People. Then in 1969 a student protest led to more permanent changes in Crystal City and the organization of *La Raza Unida Party*.[1]

Another case of organization in the mid-sixties involved the farmworker movement. The United Farm Workers Organizing Committee of the AFL-CIO worked mostly with Mexican American farm laborers in the Lower Rio Grande Valley of Texas from June 1966 to June 1967. The unionizing efforts led to bitter feelings and violence between the farmworkers and organizers on the one hand, and growers and local and state authorities on the other. Eventually the strike produced the case of *Francisco Medrano et al. v. A. Y. Allee et al.* (1972), a suit against five Texas Rangers, one sheriff, two deputy sheriffs, a justice of the peace, and a special deputy from both Dimmitt and Starr Counties. The district court issued an injunction restraining the defendants from interfering with the plaintiffs, who had suffered illegal arrests, detentions, dispersals, threats, abuse, and prosecutions.

In Northwest Texas, Mexican Americans felt increasingly inspired by the successes of the Hispanic community in the other parts of the state. Spurred on by well-established groups such as LULAC and GI Forum, Mexican Americans in Lubbock took due notice of activism elsewhere. These organizations with the aid of the AFL-CIO sponsored in June 1966 a "War on Poverty and Migrant Lubbock Conference" at Lubbock's St. Joseph Catholic Church. The conference means to aid "all people in West Texas interested in helping the poverty-stricken take advantage of various government programs." The campaign continued when in early 1967 Manuel Garza, executive director of LULAC, visited Lubbock to investigate charges of discrimination in the workplace. Without giving specific detail, Garza maintained that Mexican Americans and African Americans received less pay as well as no promotions from Lubbock employers. Garza was probably referring to an earlier strike that occurred in February of 1967. That episode involved AFL-CIO Packinghouse Workers, Local 1202, whose membership included two hundred Mexican Americans, fifteen African Americans, and all white supervisors and foremen. The strike began on February 5, 1967, against Farmers Co-op Gin, Inc., which refused to negotiate seniority rights of Mexican nos. In this case Mexican Americans lost their jobs to local African Americans who were promoted for returning to work, and to all-black crews hired from Dallas. When Local 1202 filed civil rights complaints with the EEOC, the co-op management went to Juarez, Mexico, and hired green-carders.

In this climate of mounting organization, Mexican American sanitation workers went on strike in 1968 and won a partial victory against the city of Lubbock. Tom Lara, a participant in the strike, remembered that sanitation workers had no uniforms, gloves, boots, or drinking water as did other city department workers. Lara remembered that he and fellow employees often went through the garbage looking for clothes to wear in order to avoid ruining their own clothes or boots. The lack of drinking water became a real problem for the workers, and they were forced to drink from water hoses in yards. Some Lubbock homeworkers did not like this practice and reported the workers for trespassing. Other city departments had water jugs that hung on the sides of the trucks.

Another major problem the sanitation workers faced became the lack of "Johns" at the landfill; thus, they were forced to relieve themselves behind piles of garbage. Still another issue of contention involved the practice of city official hiring Anglo foremen from the outside and overlooking Mexican American for advancement. When the walkout occurred, only the Mexican American participated while the Anglos stayed at work. The strike lasted approximately one week, and strikers asked for a 12 percent pay raise, overtime pay, and uniforms. Strikers attained uniforms and drinking water as well as portable toilets. The strikers were organized by Isidro Gutierrez, who would lead the sanitation workers in yet another strike in 1972 before eventually moving to San Antonio to organize for the Construction and Municipal Workers Union Local 1253.

Between 1968 and 1972 the AFL-CIO continued to organize workers. Under the direction of Henry Munoz, a Texas AFL-CIO Permanent Committee on Mexican American Affairs organized the Mexican American Political Action Institute (MAPAI) in March of 1970 at San Antonio. The institute was primarily funded by labor but also utilized resources from other interested groups and individuals. An advisory committee of forty members representing the eleven areas in Texas would direct the work of the institute. Isidro Gutierrez of Lubbock became a member of the advisory committee, and a steering committee was chosen from these forty members. The goal of the MAPAI became year-round political action and political education campaigns to mobilize the Mexican American vote. The MAPAI solicited the help of community leaders who were not necessarily within the ranks of labor but wished to aid in these campaigns. Educational efforts were to ensure that Mexican American votes would best serve and represent Mexican American needs and of course organized labor.

Because of the work of the MAPAI, it should have come as no surprise when on August 28, 1972, Lubbock city sanitation workers walked off the job in "protest of poverty wages." Sanitation workers asked for a 15 percent pay raise, which would increase their monthly salary from $357 to $412. Led by Isidro Gutierrez, MAPAI advisory committee member and fourteen-year veteran of the sanitation department, the workers did not go back to work for a month. The Construction and Municipal Workers Union, Local 1253, represented 75 percent of the employees in the city's public works departments. Membership numbered 350, according to union business manager Robert Mendez. Over half these members worked in the sanitation department.

Earlier, in July 1972, Mendez had appeared before the city council during a preliminary budget meeting. At the hearing Mendez had asked for a 15 percent raise for all city employees, payment for unused sick leave upon termination, and a Monday through Friday workweek. Sam Wahl, director of public works, countered that sanitation workers with seniority could take varying days off, with the first choice of Saturdays and Sundays. It became the consensus of the council that the city could not afford the 1.3 million dollars it would cost to give all city employees a 15 percent pay hike. However, the council did come up with enough money to grant pay raises for 75 percent of all city employees. Some sanitation workers did fall within that category, and if they had worked for more than a year would be eligible for a 5 percent raise.

By the end of the first week, the city of Lubbock had replaced some of the striking workers, although no decision had been made on whether protesting workers were considered terminated. City policy required that an employee be released after three days of missing work if management had not been notified of a sufficient reason for the absence. In a related development, sewage treatment plant workers stayed off their job, two men per shift, in a show of support for the sanitation workers, but despite this momentum, by Thursday, the fourth day of the strike the city council had decided there would be no 15 percent pay raise, and all but thirteen of the strikers' positions had been filled.

Analyzing the situation at the end of the first week, the *Lubbock Avalanche* found that the 154 workers that had walked off the job made from $2.11 to $2.44 an hour. Drivers made the higher wages. The average annual salary per worker was $4,652.88. Fifty-four of the workers claimed between five and nine dependents. The newspaper estimated that one man with six dependents brought home $158.77 every two weeks.

As the strike entered the second week, workers lowered their demand of a raise to 12 percent. This same week Ramsey Muniz, *Raza Unida* nominee for governor, spoke in Lubbock. He urged Mexican Americans to support the striking sanitation workers and argued that "the workers' request was reasonable and calls for a decent salary to provide food and clothes for their families." Support did not stop there. At least thirteen employees from the water, street, and water reclamation departments united with the strikers. Also, by the end of the week the Lubbock Central Labor Council offered financial aid to the workers.

The city continued to fill vacated positions. By September 9 half the workers had been replaced by new permanent employees. The city council refused to agree to any kind of pay raise, and instead pushed for containerization to lower the need for manpower. In the meantime the city encouraged employees like janitors or laborers making less money to move into the higher-paying jobs held by sanitation workers.

In the third week, the city council found replacements for all openings. Sanitation superintendent Jim Weston estimated that from 45 to 50 percent of the new employees were African American, 25 percent were Mexican American, and 25 percent were Anglo American. But the council's action generated an unexpected response from the Catholic clergy in the city. At a council hearing on September 15 lasting four hours, Lubbock priests promised to advocate a boycott among their parishioners against the municipal power service. Father Tom McGovern of Carlisle representing the Priest Senate of the Amarillo Diocese addressed the council, albeit with no success. Then Father Henry Waldo of Our Lady of Grace spoke, "We came with the faith we would be heard. We have had our say but we're not sure you've been listening. We will go to our pulpits Sunday and press for economic sanctions and ask our people en masse to switch from Lubbock Power and Light to Southwestern Public Service and not to pay the garbage service charge." Father Waldo ended by declaring. "Lubbock Power and Light has said it is people power, let's see where the real power of the people lies." A crowd of at least three hundred, comprised of sanitation workers, families, clergymen, and friends, attended the hearing in support of the strike.

True to their word, on Sunday morning Catholic priests urged their parishioners to boycott Lubbock Power and Light and not pay the garbage fee unless the city council agreed to negotiate with the strikers. They outlined a five-point program, distributed at all Lubbock churches. The program called for a utility boycott, a refusal to pay the garbage fee, a rejection of replacement workers, declarations of individual protest, and finally, making contributions to the employee protest fund, care of American State Bank. At Our Lady of Grace alone, some five hundred of about fifteen hundred people attending mass signed "switch-over cards" from Lubbock Power and Light to Southwestern Public Service. That afternoon, as the fourth week of the strike began, door-to-door campaigns began in support of a utility boycott.

By Wednesday of that week Gustavo Gaynett with the US Justice Department's Office of Community Relations arrived from the Dallas office to act as mediator. Gaynett maintained the Justice Department feared "outside agitators" might escalate the problems. He first spoke with city officials, then met with a delegation of priests. Meanwhile, the boycott continued, with a total of 250 actual customer changeovers and approximately 350 new requests. Office manager Carroll McDonald estimated that changeover requests came in at about forty a day. In addition, many customers each day threatened not to pay the two-dollar garbage fee.

At the end of the week the city council invited the sanitation workers to return to their jobs. Sanitation workers rejected the offer and presented their own plan. Finally it came down to two committees from both sides negotiating with Gaynett. The city agreed to create jobs in order to find employment for all strikers. When the positions opened up in the sanitation department, workers could return to their old positions. As to the 12 percent raise, the city would only agree to the already budgeted merit raises of 5 percent. All strikers returned to work on September 26, 1972, at the same pay. The boycott had resulted in 350 changeovers and 428 more orders awaiting the transfer to Southwestern Public Service. Once the city had agreed to put the men back to work, Catholic clergy issued a statement of approval.

The strike may be seen as a partial victory for the sanitation workers in Lubbock, since they failed to receive their demands but at least kept their jobs. In other respects the strike can be deemed as a success. Without a doubt, it united the community. The boycott implemented by the Catholic priests became a powerful force. The strike demonstrated to the entire Lubbock community that a nonviolent protest could be effective. Further, the strike launched a decade of protest and demonstration in the Lubbock *barrios*. Indeed, the sanitation workers succeeded in bringing the message to the Mexican American community that their *compañeros,* rather than looking back, should look *adelante* to the future.

Notes

This chapter originally appeared in *West Texas Historical Association Yearbook* 69 (1993): 82–88, and is reprinted with permission.

1. John Staples Shockley, *Chicano Revolt in a Texas Town* (Notre Dame: University of Notre Dame Press, 1974); *La Voz de Texas,* Lubbock, July 8, 1972; *La Prensa del Suroeste,* Lubbock, January 24, 1960, 1.

2. *Francisco Medrano et al., Plaintiffs v. A. Y. Allee et al., Defendants,* Ct. A, No. 67 B36, US District Court, Southern District of Texas, Brownsville Division, June 26, 1972.

3. *Lubbock Avalanche Journal,* June 6, 1966, March 15, 1967; Texas AFL-CIO, Mexican American Affairs, Records, 1953–1971, Series 11, Committee Hearings, 278-11-1-1, Memo from Henry Munoz to H. S. Hank Brown, October 16, 1967, Special Collections, University of Texas at Arlington.

4. Tom Lara, interview by Yolanda Romero, October 6, 1989, Lubbock, TX, Southwest Collection, Texas Tech University, Lubbock.

5. Texas AFL-CIO, Mexican American Affairs, Records, 1953–1971, Series 11, Mexican American Political Action Institute, 278-11-2-12, Special Collections, University of Texas at Arlington.

6. *Lubbock Avalanche Journal,* August 29–September 2, 1972.

7. *Lubbock Avalanche Journal,* September 4, 1972.

8. *Lubbock Avalanche Journal,* September 5–9, 1972.

9. *Lubbock Avalanche Journal,* September 14, 15, 1972.

10. *Lubbock Avalanche Journal,* September 18–23, 1972; Tom Lara interview.

11. *Lubbock Avalanche Journal,* September 25–October 5, 1972.

OUT OF THE CAR AND INTO THE FUTURE

James Duran

Roughly 19,252,215 km (or 11,962,772 mi) of the Earth's surface is paved, encouraging consistent migration.[1] As humans continue to roam the Earth, it is very likely that these numbers will increase, unfortunately, but is such activity appropriate to best manage and preserve life? Time is of the essence, and due to the prolonged human abuse and neglect of this planet's resources, the ensuing sequence of events associated with alternative courses of actions will involve intense evaluation and application of the remaining precious resources.

The aim of this essay is to highlight the positive impacts urban design and mobility have on sustainability and society. A significant representation of the international community consistently hosts discussions as to what would be the most efficient approach to preserving our finite bounty of natural resources, while establishing and maintaining a meaningful quality of life, and arguably, the most consistent conclusion involves conservation of energy.[2] Drastic changes in relation to consumption of resources were identified as a must toward the end of the twentieth century, and reiterated with the onset of the twenty-first century.[3] Yet in 2016, unified international agreements focused on implementation of effective conservation policies and regulations, designed to protect ecological systems around the world, are still cause for political gridlock and conflict.

Data collected from 1997 to 2007 suggest that the United States had been the world's largest consumer of energy and resources.[4] The People's Republic of China now leads the world in this category; however, the United States is positioned as a close second while our population and political representatives collectively struggle to redirect our dependency on fossil fuels. When scientific communities are asked to consider in which capacity individuals can actively engage in to preserve our planet, reducing emissions released into the atmosphere is often at the top of their list.[5] This is where design and infrastructure come into play.

To maximize the impact of the relationship that exists between these two systems, we should appreciate that environmental sustainability depends on both design and infrastructure to be enhanced simultaneously, and should be engaged as quickly as possible. However, part of the complication in the delivery of acceptable solutions may be in defining part of the subjected process, and that would be mobility. Definitions, just as interpretations, can vary from city to city and from one country to another.

Per the United Nations, mobility is: "a key dynamic of urbanization, and the associated infrastructure invariably shapes the urban form—the spatial imprint defined by roads, transport systems, spaces, and buildings—of cities."[6] What is thoroughly disappointing is the mobility options presented in the United States, especially when compared on an international scale. The U.S. Economic Office of Foreign Relations has deemed infrastructure and transportation as major factors in developing and maintaining economic prosperity in the near future.[7] We should also consider what is being done to improve conditions for all affected. Is the collective governing body in the United States doing their best to implement sustainable changes, or do they resort to and apply political polarization tactics to block and allocate funds away from truly enhancing infrastructure development?

From 2000 to 2008, dozens of legislative actions were passed, many of those without including specific dollar amounts being allocated toward completion of transportation projects.[8] It was extremely difficult to identify a single transportation project that specifically supported initiatives beyond highway construction, which may lead reviewing parties to wonder why elected officials who were concerned with improving conditions associated with transportation, and mobility, failed to mention alternatives to highway construction. Advanced societies around the world, such as Amsterdam, Copenhagen, London, Madrid, Paris, Tokyo, and Vienna, have enhanced their quality of life by funding the establishment and development of extremely convenient transit systems, not necessarily roads, to move people across broad and expansive terrain. It wasn't until the 111th Congress that "Transportation" legislation began to mention alternative transportation projects that went beyond highway construction, and included limits on spending.[9]

From 2009 to 2015, the collective legislative branch of government has sponsored roughly 10 bills that have been signed by President Barack Obama, but most of these bills fail to clearly identify any specific amount of fiscal resources that would be allocated toward any of the aforementioned transportation projects we so desperately need. Instead, Congress has suggested fiscal spending ceilings be set in the amount of $182.6 billion to fund multiple highway projects across the country.[10]

To justify the perspective of considering alternatives to paving the planet with highways, legislative bill after legislative bill (HR 3819; HR 2353; HR 3996; HR 5021; etc.) go on to suggest that alternative mass transit projects travel down the route of formula grant proposals to suggest what options would be best to consider for the years ahead.[11] On legislative action, S.808: Surface Transportation Board Reauthorization Act of 2015; Section 3 through Section 5, federal policy suggests that a special board be formed, apart from the U.S. Department of Transportation (DOT) to provide alternative suggestions related to transportation, to the DOT, Congress, the president, and hopefully the impacted population (no mention of the public being briefed; as a matter of fact S.808 suggests this "special board" be authorized to meet privately, and not have to share minutes with anyone, unless private discussions include suggestions related to DOT mass transit initiatives).[12]

What should be most alarming about these already executed legislative actions, specifically S.808, is this transportation board of "experts" is no longer restricted to transportation experts, instead has been expanded to include anyone who has standing knowledge in the transportation area, transportation regulation, or economic regulation (Section 4). S.808 goes on to allow up to two additional people who have professional or business experience in private sectors. A private citizen with an extensive background in the agriculture industry can now be invited and authorized as a functioning and contributing member to an independent, regulatory agency, hosting private discussions related to surface transportation alternatives in this country (Section 5).

Part of the reason this is taking place may be due to the multitude of businesses and industries responsible for and benefitting from covering our planet's surface area to accommodate vehicles. Government administrators have reduced the purchasing price of massive lots that encourages and allows investors to proceed with establishing car lots, almost entirely business-related operations.[13] But perhaps more of the average citizens should consider the larger impact human engineering has on our natural living environments. Transportation, and moving around a city, has tremendous impact on the human psyche, physical well-being, and the surrounding environment.[14] The average citizen also needs to change their approach and attitudes associated with transit. Until larger segments of society decide to look at transit differently, it will be very challenging to convince taxpayers, voters, and riders that transit is one of the best options for getting people from point A to points B, C, and D.

The argument can be made that cities across the United States were designed to provide separation from one another. From early colonialist days, early immigrants recognized vast territories yet to be discovered, which presented an open space to freely create specialized communities where groups of humans could collectively occupy territory, share some sort of common initiative to sustain life for an extended period of time, and specialize in specific areas that would allow fiscal stability via trade. But as societies became more and more advanced (ideas and approaches to life were released and challenged in groups), and civilizations began to interact with each other at higher frequencies, urban cores became more and more dense.[15]

Acquiring mineral resources, and then trading these resources and other goods with the larger community propelled transit systems to develop at an accelerated rate. And when executed with precision and purpose, advanced cities certainly do receive a return on their investment in the form of increased productivity and tourism.[16] Considering these

© goga18128/Shutterstock.com

factors, why is the recognizable collection of highly efficient, regional transit systems concentrated in Europe? For the sake of the planet, let us now consider North American modes of transit. The largest population in North America, in terms of humans registering to a single nationality as well as recorded noncitizens, would be that of the United States.

It is worth considering expenses allocated toward owning and operating vehicles versus not. Arguments can be made for eras in which vehicles were being grossly underpriced, which can often be perpetuated by ever-expanding consumer markets, that now include virtual arenas (e.g., Craigslist and Cars.com).[17] These markets lend themselves to a car culture that can easily be identified with the United States. Compound this heightened desire of gaining possession of a personal people mover with the possibility of crossing once vast geographic territories, metropolitan cities, and states that neighbor each other to create the collective regions that represent the United States, leaving the able consumer increasingly dependent on all variables involved in this relationship.

Commuting over 40 or 60 miles round trip, *daily*, is unfortunately common place for hundreds of thousands of people across the United States. Per an *Urban Mobility Scorecard* completed in 2015, Washington, DC, has the highest record of "gridlock" with an average of 82 hours spent in traffic per driver per year.[18] Our nation's capital is followed closely by Los Angeles at 80 hours, San Francisco at 78 hours, New York at 74 hours, and San Jose at 67 hours. In cities with intense gridlock traffic, drivers are advised to double their commute time during "rush-hour traffic" to be sure to maintain time commitments.

Besides time that is being lost, in a society that very much recognizes the value of each second, our health is the next aspect of life being compromised via the dependency upon the automobile. According to the U.S. Department of Transportation, a study conducted in Atlanta, GA, found that for each additional hour spent in an automobile, obesity rates would increase by 6 percent.[19] Compound this health concern with increased particulate matter being spewed out of automotive exhaust pipes, then living organisms should consider rates of respiratory complications and death associated with air pollution.[20] Three billion gallons of fuel is lost when commuters are stuck in traffic.[21] Sitting in traffic is not typically considered commuters' favorable activity to engage in. Some could even argue that traffic can be stressful. This traffic-related stress can also be attributed to increased heart conditions that would compromise people's overall health.[22]

The most recognizable changes for resolving many of the aforementioned situations would best include collaborative efforts from the private sector and public sector. This would be the most difficult process in a culture that has officially adopted the automobile as the primary means of transportation. But this current course of action is absolutely unsustainable! Our current "leadership" knows this; however, they continue to direct the masses in the opposite direction of a sustainable future. Yes, the responsibility now lies on the adult population's course of action, and now we need to wake up and insist on changes, otherwise time, energy, and resources will continue to be depleted. The solution requires the general population to increase their general knowledge in relation to and attitudes toward: (1) commuting, (2) city planning and land development, and (3) voting.

Economic analysis should include comparisons between vehicular travel and public transit travel. Arguably, an extremely enjoyable, liberating, and physically beneficial mode of transportation is not being endorsed the way it should to have the impact it can: bicycling. It does not help when land management and urban design models

© Anton_Ivanov/Shutterstock.com

fail to include practical concepts, such as a bicycle lane or bicycle rack. Instead, new developments span miles into new subdivisions, isolating residents from inter-action with each other due to dependence on traditional means of transit, namely, the automobile.

"Civilized" American societies deserve more options than what we are receiving, and it should not be beyond our financial limitations to provide alternatives to getting around. As more components of a "pedestrian-friendly city" become common prac-tice and integrated into American urban design, we may begin encouraging the shift from the automobile to a healthier method of engaging with our natural environment, the bicycle. With this less threatening mode of transit, public service administrators should also notice less wear and tear on roads, allowing municipal, state, and federal governments more opportunities to apply millions of tax payer dollars to either: 1) pay off outstanding balances accrued up to that point; 2) save for later use; or 3) invest in economic development projects throughout cities across the country.

Mentioned government systems may also reconsider appropriations allocated toward parking garages, business parking lots, and parking spaces in urban core centers. As urban planners and designers reconsider these almost immediately nec-essary structures, communities could potentially have architectural "makeovers" with buildings that visually invite humans into public spaces, rather than forcing them to focus on locating space to park their cars. Attractive, sustainable design is critically important to focus proper investment of resources, especially when timing is of the essence.

The changing environmental conditions have even gone so far as to suggest that as sea levels rise, they will take control of cities, forcing residents to evacuate and migrate for an extended period of time.[23] Such migrations will very likely apply more pressure onto urban centers across the country and around the world. With a lack of transportation options throughout the USA, increased human presence will very likely be immediately noticeable in the form of increased congestion at all hours of the day, impacting quality of life.

It can be argued that alternatives to commuting and transportation can and should assist with our current situation of dwindling resources and environmental imbalance, and to make significant changes communities across the globe can benefit from, mas-sive transportation projects can and should be seriously considered to receive the fiscal support required to cover comprehensive expenses. Organization for Economic Co-operation and Development (OECD) has suggested a process to decarbonize delivery of products to consumers that may help reduce the amount of carbon dioxide released into the atmosphere by 23% over the next 35 to 50 years.[24] This effort is known to be on the shared path of carbon neutrality, and was initiated into effect at the International Transport Forum on May 19, 2016.

Agreeable messages are delivered when the Executive Office endorses forward-thinking transportation projects such as those associated with American Recovery and Reinvestment Act (ARRA) of 2009, to focus on roughly 2,800 transportation projects that go beyond highway construction, in all 50 states. However, congress continues to generate and sponsor legislative action that seems to ignore scientif-ic reasoning that indicates traditional human behavior is destroying this planet's ecological systems. It is imperative that the political powers, operating in the

© T photography/Shutterstock.com

United States, revert from paving the planet to make the movement of humans and materials more convenient.

Humans living in the United States can actively participate in urban development that would neutralize and alleviate heightened stress variables naturally associated with migration patterns by drafting progressive urban cityscapes to include mixed-use developments; comprehensive transit options; and limited growth of the traditional road, or highway, incorporated to facilitate an easier path for the private automobile owner. With the inclusion of "smart growth," pedestrians can re-establish positive connections within societies.[25] Scientists should recognize improvements to the quality of air in heavily populated cities, along with a reduction of ambient noise associated with traffic.[26]

People who more often use public transit are more likely to "connect" with their natural surroundings as opposed to individuals who choose to remain confined to an automobile.[27] Scientists should also notice a decrease in fatalities coming from automobiles; auto accidents should also be reduced; and police should notice a drop in crime related to automobile theft or moving violations (e.g., speeding, running through traffic signals, and reckless driving); coincidentally, automobile fatalities are recognized as the number one threat to life for millennials.[28]

Radical changes associated with such planning and design should include increased human interaction, which would also encourage appreciation for others in efforts to re-establish a positive sense of community. As appreciation for others increases, so should the appreciation of our environment. With alternative urban design, humans might be "forced" to walk, bicycle, or use enhanced public transit systems, collectively slowing down our daily routines so that we can appreciate this human experience a bit more.

Opposing viewpoints may prove to be costly beyond immediate comprehension as international observers can base their own human course of action off this failure to do what is necessary. Accommodating automobile traffic to move across the planet is the most expensive, most resource-intensive, and least sustainable method of moving people and commodities across the planet known to man.[29] Even marketing specialists can help preserve our national security a bit more if they could introduce slogans that encouraged adoption, and application, of public transit or transit alternatives (e.g., bicycling) more appealing. We could encourage celebrities, athletes, and public figures to come out and endorse such endeavors as "cool!"[30]

Why do government systems decide to not apply as much resources as possible to allow their constituents the freedom and security necessary to fill the void associated with a mobility gap?[31] Is it a disservice to taxpayers to apply trillions of dollars into one specific area or category to resolve a transportation problem expecting different results? Are the Unites States' "elected officials" placing humanity's collective interests second to their own? What can be done to challenge the "decided" course for the future? These and the ensuing scenarios deserve to be considered as we continue to struggle and establish a life away from the automobile.

With the evolution of species, adaptive civilizations around the world extended their survival skills after mastering the concept of conservation and mobility.[32] Whether a solitary entity from a tribe, or a group of organisms from a more extensive ecosystem, consuming an overabundance of energy from the core can be detrimental to the overall existence of the nucleus or base. Similar concepts can be applied to human migration: there is strength in numbers; thus, it may be in the best interest of the group to travel in packs. It is crucial to plan accordingly, with consideration of how human action impacts engaged environments; how broad and expansive our occupation of land becomes; how we choose to move about; and our interaction with each other.

Life has a way of resolving situations between gluttonous cells that consistently absorb energy and resources without positively replenishing the natural balance that is known to be in coexistence with other living organisms. That which consumes more than can be produced shall be exterminated or exiled from the group to preserve the well-being of that which remains. That which threatens survival will be forced to fend for themselves. Complications that face modern civilizations today will involve extermination or exile. The reality humans are dealing with now begs the questions: (1) how many of us will fight to avoid complete annihilation to remain occupants of an ever-evolving planet; (2) how many will remain apathetic, expediting the extinction process; and (3) who will be among the few that avoid this scenario by fleeing the planet?

Should Americans and their collective "leaders" continue down the traditional path of automobile dependency, we will lose the environmental, social, and economic sustainability competition. Transportation methods in the United States have evolved tremendously: from application of horses in early settlements as the nation was establishing transportation networks from one colony to another, to the now almost complete reliance upon automated vehicles. However, it is imperative that we recognize and reduce the collection of resources being applied to facilitate the "modern" movement networks, as collectively they represent an express path with coordinates leading to the end of the world.

Many of the transportation alternatives suggested would initiate economic growth, while presenting and emphasizing time be used to appreciate the finer details in life. Transportation alternatives in the United States would send a definitive message to the rest of the world that we care about preserving life: from accidental auto-related mortality to international conflict with objectives of obtaining more physical resources. With an alternative course of action, and thousands of lives saved, we could encourage more humans to become involved in the process of negotiating for a more peaceful, holistically sustainable, and comfortable existence. Here's to a glorious future, and the stories yet to be told!

Notes

1. "Roadways." *Central Intelligence Agency: The World Factbook.* 1999–2016. www.cia.gov/library/publications/resources/the-world-factbook/fields/2085.html. Accessed 15 September 2016.

2. "Sustainable Development Goals: 17 Goals to Transform Our World." United Nations. www.un.org/sustainabledevelopment. Accessed 11 September 2016.

3. Moss, R. H., R. T. Watson, and M. C. Zinyowera. *The Regional Impacts of Climate Change: An Assessment of Vulnerability.* Intergovernmental Panel on Climate Change. Cambridge, UK: Cambridge University Press, 1998.

4. *Global Energy Statistical Yearbook 2016.* Enerdata. https://yearbook.enerdata.net. Accessed 18 September 2016.

5. Olivieri, John. "New Federal Data Show Transportation Sector Now the Largest Source of Carbon Pollution in the United States, First Time in Nearly 40 Years." United States Public Interest Research Group. August 2016. www.uspirg.org/news/usp/new-federal-data-show-transportation-sectornow-largest-source-carbon-pollution-united. Accessed 11 September 2016.

6. "Mobility." United Nations Habitat. https://unhabitat.org/urban-themes/mobility/. Accessed 28 August 2016.

7. Markovich, Steven J. "Transportation Infrastructure: Moving America." Council on Foreign Relations. October 2014. www.cfr.org/infrastructure/transportation-infrastructure-movingamerica/p18611. Accessed 28 August 2016.

8. Govtrack.us. Congressional sessions tracked from 2001 to 2015. Focused on "Transportation." Accessed 10 September 2016.

9. Ibid.

10. Ibid.

11. Ibid.

12. Ibid.

13. Cervero, Robert. *The Transit Metropolis: A Global Inquiry.* Washington, DC: Island Press, 1998.

14. Crawford, J. H. *Carfree Cities.* International Press, 2000.

15. Glaeser, Edward. *Triumph of the City.* Penguin Group, 2011.

16. Ibid.

17. Crawford, J. H. *Carfree Cities.* International Press, 2000.

18. https://tti.tamu.edu/2015/08/26/traffic-gridlock-sets-new-records-for-traveler-misery/

19. https://www.transportation.gov/mission/health/vmt-capita.

20. Fischlowitz-Roberts, Bernie. "Plan B Updates." Earth Policy Institute. 17 September 2002.

21. Ibid.

22. Kan, Haidong, Gerardo Hiess, Kathryn M. Rose, Eric A. Whitsel, Fred Lurmann, et al. *Prospective Analysis of Traffic Exposure to Risk Factor for Incident Coronary Heart Disease: The Atherosclerosis Risk in Communities (ARIC) Study*. Research Triangle Park, Durham, NC: Environmental Health Perspectives, 2008.

23. "Global Warming Impacts." Union of Concerned Scientists. www.ucsusa.org/our-work/globalwarming/science-and-impacts/global-warming-impacts#.V-nbeu-EDIU. Accessed 17 September 2016.

24. Chateau, Jean, Christina Clapp, Rob Dellink, Eliza Lanzi, Bertrand Magne, Virginie Marchal, Jasper van Vliet, and Detlef van Vuuren. "OECD Environmental Outlook to 2050: Climate Change Chapter." OECD.org. November 2011. https://www.oecd.org/env/cc/49082173.pdf. Accessed 10 September 2016.

25. Grescoe, Taras. Strap Hanger. New York, NY: Times Books, 2012.

26 Dennis, Kingsley, and John Urry. *After the Car*. Malden, MA: Polity Press, 2009.

27. Crawford, J. H. *Carfree Cities*. International Press, 2000.

28. Furness, Zack. *One Less Car*. Philadelphia, PA: Temple University Press, 2010.

29. Crawford, J. H. *Carfree Cities*. International Press, 2000.

30. Furness, Zack *One Less Car*. Philadelphia, PA: Temple University Press, 2010.

31. O'Toole, Randle. *Gridlock*. Washington, DC: The Cato Institute, 2009.

32. Darwin, Charles. *Origin of the Species*. J. Murray, 1859.

FARM TO FREEDOM: IN OUR GARDEN, AFTER THE WAR

Roy Vũ

Homeland within a Home

During the Việt Nam War, the government of the Republic of Việt Nam (RVN), commonly referred to as South Việt Nam or Southern Việt Nam, issued postage stamps of fruits and vegetables that were widely grown and consumed throughout the country. The beloved (yet awful-tasting in my opinion) trái khổ qua or bitter melon was depicted on the 1.50 piastres (đồng) stamp.[1] The soursop (mãng cầu) was canonized on a 3.00 piastres stamp and the cashew apple (trại điều) on the 50-cent piastre stamp.[2] These vegetables, immortalized on stamps, are still grown half a world away by Vietnamese Americans, gardening and toiling under the Texas sun. For the Vietnamese diaspora, the war, which ended 41 years ago with thousands of refugees desperately fleeing their homeland, remains both a distant nightmare and a fresh memory, a reminder of what was destroyed . . . and recreated.

In comparison to the scale of war and resettlement, what has been recreated may at first appear miniscule, inconsequential, and irrelevant. However, seeds, soil, sun, and water, mixed with physical labor, persistence, ingenuity, and pursuit of life's "rich rewards," have, without a doubt, helped connect Vietnamese Americans to their homeland. The products of their labor—a cornucopia of vegetables, fruits, and herbs—reward the growers with an opportunity to provide a lifetime of repasts that are shared with family and friends. These meals bind loved ones, communities, and generations.

For many Vietnamese Americans, their home gardens are places of sanctuary and healing. They nurture the mind, body, and soul. What grows in Việt Nam continues to be grown in the backyards of Vietnamese Americans, creating a transnational link via shared foodways. Such strong personal ties to food have survived through wars, refuge, and resettlement and open a gateway to memories of a bygone era and a bygone country—Southern Việt Nam.

Purpose: "This Is an Effort to Preserve and Extend the Traditions of Our Ancestors"

Nguyễn Văn Nam[3] learned how to garden while growing up in Việt Nam, helping his mother in their front and backyards.[4] Mr. Nguyễn recalls: "Back home in North Việt Nam, when I was a little boy, my father was the only one working. My mother stayed home, taking care of the house, watching the children, going to the market nearby to get food, preparing the meals, and working in the garden when she had time. . . . We had a big backyard with fruit trees and a bigger front yard for vegetables. . . . When my sister and I came home from school, we tried to do our homework and study our lessons first. If we still had time, we went to the front yard to help mom. I learned from mom how to use the shovel, hoe, and rake. I also learned how to plant different kinds of vegetables and how to take care of them."

"In 1975, I came to the United States," writes Mr. Nguyễn "I was sponsored by an American family in Covington, Kentucky. Here, I got a job teaching French at a high school." Six years later, Nam got in contact with old friends whom he worked with in the Catholic Confederation in Việt Nam. He recounts: "Most of these guys suggested that we regroup to try preserving our culture and tradition. We decided to take Houston as our first choice. It is in Houston that we had permission from KPFT (Houston PBS station affiliate) to broadcast a weekly program in Vietnamese. My wife and I moved to Houston in 1981 to join the Lạc Việt group." He and his wife, Thi, and their children eventually moved to Cypress, a suburb in northwest Houston, where they began their own home garden about 20 years ago.[5] Nam recollects: "When we moved to Houston, we met a few old friends who own several nurseries around town. They helped me to plant a few vegetables in the backyard both for fun and for food." Prof. Nguyễn, or Thầy Nam, as his colleagues, students, community leaders, and friends affectionately and respectfully call him these days, has taught Vietnamese language courses at the University of Houston for over a decade now.

Thầy Nam enjoys cultivating his home garden not only for the food it produces, but also to see the plants grow each day—plants such as water spinach (rau muống), spearmint (húng lùi), okra (đậu bắp), and winter melon (bí đao). But more importantly, Thầy Nam believes that gardening helps the Vietnamese in the United States maintain a part of their tradition. Thầy Nam told me: "This is an effort to preserve and extend the traditions of our ancestors. The Vietnamese, when leaving their homeland, promise to themselves to preserve and to develop their traditions and culture. To preserve and develop the traditions and culture doesn't [just] include books, songs . . . but also [a] way to live such as planting and eating [traditionally grown vegetables]."[6]

Joy: "Gardening Makes Life More Beautiful!"

At the tail end of the second wave of Vietnamese exodus, Hoàng Quang and Nguyễn Lan resettled in the United States in 1985.[7] Mr. Hoàng learned to garden as a four-year-old child growing up in Việt Nam.[8] His wife, Lan, started gardening soon after they relocated to Pearland, Texas, where they currently live. Since then, they have maintained a lush, immaculate home garden that features an abundance of vegetables, fruit trees, and herbs that would rival the produce section of a neighborhood grocery store. The couple grows fruits and vegetables such as mustard greens (dưa cái), chili peppers (cay ớt), papaya (đu đủ), satsuma oranges (cam satsuma), kumquats (cây quất cảnh), bitter melon, Fuyu persimmons (trái hồng), and various herbs.

Their son, Son Hoàng, recently recounted a more detailed and heart-wrenching story of his parents that is not uncommon among Vietnamese refugees. Son Hoàng recalls his parents' remarkable journey from courage and desperation to separation and deep sorrow to reunion and absolute joy:

"My parents were a young couple with an eighteen-month-old child (me), at the end of the Việt Nam War.[9] In the midst of the chaos leading up to April 30, 1975, my dad and relatives made the decision to escape through Tân Sơn Nhứt Airport. He and his family were all military personnel, and he himself was a pilot. . . . The next day, they came to the airport with my uncle's family because he had secured a military lift out of the country. . . . My mom and I got in but my dad was stuck because he left his badges at home. (Military personnel all changed into civilian clothes to avoid being targeted.) After a long while, my mom became frantic because she could not see my dad coming in. At the same time, I was having a high fever. She then decided to come back out to find my dad so that we all could stay together no matter what.

What she did not know was my dad had bribed the guards with his motorcycle to enter the gate.[10] That is where the two of them were separated and lost from one another, leading to a decade long separation with limited contact and knowledge of the whereabouts of each other. Both of them suffered from severe depression, and mom was on the verge of suicide to have lost her young husband and most of her own family. What kept her going was me and the comfort of having my maternal grandmother in Biên Hoà.

When my dad and relatives finally arrived to Camp Pendleton, California (one of the four makeshift Vietnamese refugee camps under U.S. Operation New Life), they were separated when the family split everyone up based on the availability of host families . . . my dad found a Hispanic host family in Houston, Texas.[11] My parents did not know how to contact each other for years. . . . In Houston, my dad became a machinist and gradually rose to the rank of management. He finally managed to contact my mom after almost eight years and then quickly sponsored me and my mom to reunite in Houston.

My mom, on the other hand, had a sister in Paris who left Việt Nam in the 1950s and was working on the documentation to sponsor me, my mom, and my grandma to France.[12] We had already received the paperwork to leave the country when my maternal grandmother died and my parents finally reconnected via mail. The reunification process to the United States was expedited thanks to the existing paperwork to leave Việt Nam for France. My mom and I finally met my dad in July 1984. It was the first time (except when I was a baby) I met my father.

Prior to bringing my mom and me to the United States, my dad purchased 12 acres of land in Pearland, which was then subdivided among some of his Vietnamese co-workers, to establish a small Vietnamese village.[13] We lived in a mobile home on two acres of land. My dad inherited my grandfather and great grandfather's love of working on the land. . . . When my dad purchased the land in Pearland, he already had an idea of what he wanted to do. During my early years of living on the land, we had a small farm of hundreds of chickens, a few swans, a dozen rabbits, generations of dogs, a few cats, and one peacock.

My dad grew all sorts of trees: pears, peaches, persimmons, etc.[14] On the other hand, my mom did not take up planting until we moved off the land and into a Pearland subdivision. I guess to her, planting and managing a 7000 square feet lot is much easier than two acres. Since retirement, they have been planting and growing both decorative and practical gardens, each year improving on their techniques and craft. They now are able to cross-breed the fruits and vegetables to achieve the sweetest kumquats and graft plants to produces seedless oranges. . . . Life in Pearland became home for both of my parents because they never imagined living elsewhere."

As for Son's parents, his mother, Lan, enjoys thinking of these beautiful plants as the product of her hard work and appreciates that the fresh produce strengthens and improves their health.[15] His father, Quang, strongly believes that gardening helps him "remember the past," connecting them with their previous life in Việt Nam. They both find gardening a nurturing daily activity that not only reduces stress but provides a connection to nature. Quang explains: "Gardening makes you live close to nature and makes life more beautiful!" Lan adds: "It's also good for our relationship because it gives us things to do together."[16]

Memory: "A Greater Sense of Our Mother Country . . . "

When the Communists took over Sài Gòn in 1975, my parents and older siblings fled from Việt Nam. After resettling at Fort Chaffee, Arkansas, one of the four refugee resettlement camps, they eventually made a secondary migration to Houston. My father, Vũ Kiến An Quan, who learned to garden from his parents while in Việt Nam,[17] told me, "In Việt Nam, people work hard with their hands, watching vegetables and fruits and [the] weather."[18] When we had our own house and yard in the United States, he and my mother, Trần Thị Diem Dung, began to garden once more. They planted okra, persimmons, mint leaves, chili peppers, and more.

Growing up in our modest abode in southeast Houston, I had a cursory interest in what my parents grew. I neither understood nor gave much thought as to why they would grow opo squash (trái bầu) and peach trees. At the time, I could not exactly comprehend what they were practicing was considered "garden-to-table" since planting fruit trees and vegetables was a daily, *passé* ritual for them. I did not truly appreciate their recreational and practical gardening to be organic and healthy in more ways than one. As a young adult, what began to pique my curiosity was that even though our family printing business, Houston Vàng, was struggling, and we had to live rather frugally, my parents continued to grow fruit trees, chili peppers, and opo squash and yet give away most of what they cultivated to relatives, friends, and fellow churchgoers. At the time, I was completely unaware of the communal act that they shared with other Vietnamese Houstonians. Like so many of their fellow kinsmen and kinswomen—in spite of our working class struggles—my parents were always willing to literally share the fruits of their labor with others.

So what was their reward? For certain, my parents take great pleasure and a little pride watching their herbs, vegetables, and fruit trees grow. For them, gardening is not a business venture, but a leisure activity to enjoy. Like Thầy Nam, Hoàng Quang, and Nguyễn Lan, they give their fresh produce to their children, relatives, and friends. But maybe more importantly, my father believes that gardening gives them a greater sense of our mother country."[19]

Spirituality: "Vietnamese Spirit into My Mouth . . . "

Like my parents and thousands of other Vietnamese refugees, Trần Thị Lùng left Việt Nam after the Communist takeover of Sài Gòn. In the chaotic last days of the Việt Nam War, Lùng and her husband, Phạm Minh Thú, were separated when Thú decided to go back home to find and retrieve his mother.[20] As their situation became even more dire and desperate, Lùng and her children had no choice but to depart with friends after waiting for as long as possible for her husband to return to them. She and her children finally departed with friends and strangers on a boat, desperately trying to escape from the Vietnamese Communists. Lùng and her children were refugees, and she did not know when she would ever see her husband again. Instead, they began their journey as traumatized and anguished yet relieved and determined strangers coming to America, in search of a new homeland while mourning what was lost from the war.

After leaving the Fort Chaffee refugee camp and making a secondary migration to the Dallas–Ft. Worth area, Lùng and her family moved into a subsidized apartment in Duncanville, Texas, in 1976.[21] Here, Lùng learned to garden from a Vietnamese friend. At first, she planted herbs and chili peppers in a little plot next to the apartment that was usually used for landscaping.[22]

In 1991, after more than fifteen years of separation, Lùng reunited with her husband, Thú, and his mother. Thú had been detained by Vietnamese Communists and forced to live in re-education camps because of his political affiliation with the Southern Việt Nam government. A year after their reunion, the family relocated to a Duncanville home with a sizeable backyard. The spacious yard made Lùng happy because she could expand her garden and plant persimmon trees and more vegetables. In 2003, the family moved once more, resettling in a new subdivision in Grand Prairie, where Lùng and her husband now grow a variety of mints, perilla (tía tô), lemongrass (sà), chives (hẹ), cilantro (ngò), spinach (rau mồng tơi), luffa (mướp), bitter melon, and summer squash (bầu).

Despite some challenges to gardening in the heat of the Texas sun as well as the time and labor spent, Lùng believes it is a worthwhile endeavor. She loves all the vegetables, herbs, and fruits that she grows. "When I put Vietnamese veggies, herbs, and fruits in my mouth that is very special to me," said Ms. Trần. "When I eat them . . . I feel like I have Vietnamese spirit in my mouth . . . they all taste so good to me . . . especially the food from my garden." She believes that "Gardening is for relaxation after a long day working or to see the new day with new things growing in the backyard. But the best is [to] share . . . with our friends and relatives."[23]

Conclusion

Not that a flag emblazoned with a bitter melon would ever supplant the Republic of Việt Nam flag with its three, red horizontal stripes symmetrically bisecting a yellow background, but for many Vietnamese refugees, gardens become an essential grounding connection to their lost homeland. Such gardens not only serve as a small reminder of a terrible war and a distant past but also evoke the roots they established in their new country. While these things may fade and escape from memory, these gardens help nurture and heal the mind, body, and spirit of Vietnamese American home gardeners.

In their post-war resettlement in the United States, Vietnamese Americans have found a new home—once perceived as temporary, but now, for most, permanent. Yet memories never truly die. What is practiced by generation after generation becomes habitual, part of the culture—even when your homeland is now a ghost land. For Vietnamese Americans, the common praxis includes not only an anticommunist narrative, but also foodways such as growing the food they cherish. Such a transnational linkage becomes a portal to past memories of taste, smell, sight, and touch—memories from the war, as well as from before and after the war. Now, these memories, a little piece of their homeland, have been planted and nurtured in the Texas soil by Vietnamese American home gardeners. When they harvest, share, and consume the bounty they produce in their home gardens, they share a sliver of homeland; they discover and recreate both a sanctuary—from the traumas of war, exile, and acculturation—and a new homeland. By replanting their roots here in the Texas soil, and cultivating bountiful home gardens, Vietnamese Americans cultivate ties to a Việt Nam they remember so that future generations may enjoy the fruits of their labor.

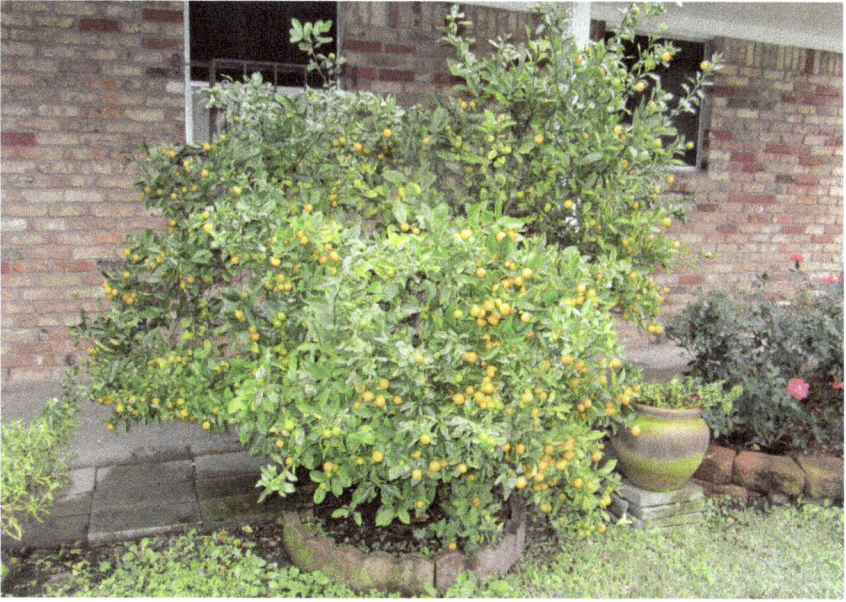

Kumquat tree. Used in candied kumquat (mứt tắc). Houston, TX. Anquân K. Vũ and Đung Trần. (*Photo by Ngọc Vũ.*)

Luffa/loofah squash. Used in Vietnamese luffa with shrimp stir fry (mướp tôm xào). Houston, TX. Quang V. Hoàng and Lan T. Nguyễn. (*Photo by Son Hoàng.*)

Green papayas. Used in Vietnamese green papaya salad (gỏi đu đủ). Pearland, TX. Quang V. Hoàng and Lan T. Nguyễn. (*Photo by Son Hoàng.*)

Bitter melon. Used in bitter melon soup (canh mướp dắng or sometimes called canh khổ qua). Pearland, TX. Quang V. Hoang and Lan T. Nguyễn. (*Photo by Son Hoàng.*)

Fuzzy winter squash/melon. Used in Vietnamese winter melon soup (canh bi). Grand Prairie, TX. Lùng Trần. (*Photo by Điệp Besaw.*)

Notes

1. Collection of Vietnamese Stamps and Currency, MS-SEA 052, Box 1, Folder 3 (Irvine, CA: The UC Irvine Libraries Special Collections and Archives, January 22, 2015).

2. Ibid.

3. According to Vietnamese tradition, the person's last or family name is stated first, followed by the middle name, and finally the first name. To avoid confusion, names are quoted under Vietnamese formality throughout the text. The author has chosen to state Vietnamese names in accordance with American standards only in the end notes.

4. Prof. Nam Van Nguyễn, interview surveyed by author, Houston, TX, September 20, 2015.

5. Ibid.

6. Ibid.

7. Mr. Quang Hoàng and Ms. Lan Nguyễn, interview surveyed by author, Houston, TX, September 6, 2015.

8. Ibid.

9. Mr. Son Hoàng, interview surveyed by author, Houston, TX, February 21, 2016.

10. Ibid.

11. Ibid.

12. Ibid.

13. Ibid.

14. Ibid.

15. Mr. Quang Hoàng and Ms. Lan Nguyễn, interview surveyed by author, Houston, TX, September 6, 2015.

16. Ibid.

17. Mr. An Quan Kiến Vũ, interview surveyed by author, Houston, TX, September 27, 2015.

18. Ibid.

19. Ibid.

20. Ms. Lùng Thi Trấn, interview surveyed by author, Grand Prairie, TX, September 7, 2015.

21. Ibid.

22. Ibid.

23. Ibid.

WE ARE NOT ALL MEXICANS: THE GROWTH OF THE LATINO POPULATION IN IRVING, TEXAS, 1970–2000

Yolanda Romero

The site or plat for Irving was filed by J. O. Schultz and Otis Brown on May 27, 1903, but it would not be until December 19 when the sale of plots began and future residents became land owners. Rock Island railroad service had come to Irving on December 1. Fifty years before this, Comanches lived in the area known as District 8 of Dallas County. George Alfred, known as "Indian George," spoke about life in District 8 in an interview done in the 1970s. Over 2,000 Comanches led by their warrior chief, White Eagle, hunted buffalo until circumstances forced them to turn to cattle. Alfred also spoke about the white settlers, like the Schultzs who became great friends. Mrs. Schultz taught the Native American women how to make biscuits, a favorite of their husbands; she would later be made an honorary member of the tribe. There were also other families, like the David Caster family; the Caster family cabin is preserved in the Irving Heritage Center. There were dozens of other families that did move into Irving. Of the families, not one was Hispanic. The only Hispanics in the area lived along the Trinity River Bottoms and worked on the local farms; there were also railroad workers who followed the railroad.[1]

In 1910, the Luis Ponce family would be the first Hispanic family to move to Irving and become permanent residents. The three boys all graduated from Irving High School known as Little Red and worked until they joined the military and fought in World War II. From 1910 to 1940, the Ponce family was joined in Irving by other Hispanic families; the Fernandez, the Santoscoys, and the Francos, together with the Martinez, were all early residents. For the most part in the early years, the parents kept to themselves, but the children did get involved in school activities. In the late twentieth century, Francisco Franco would run and win the election to the school board, and Roy Santoscoy, Jr. would be elected in the early twenty-first century to the City Council.[2] Irving underwent many changes from the 1940s to the 1960s. World War II veterans came back eager to begin their lives and invest time in making Irving a better city. Irving, known as a "bedroom community" before the war, began to grow into a thriving town. The University of Dallas opened in 1956 and the building of the Texas Stadium, home of the Dallas Cowboys, began and was completed in 1971. In the mid-1960s, African Americans were finally allowed to rent an apartment in Irving, but changes did not come quickly to the daily lives of minorities.

There were still problems of racism and discrimination for people of color, but for Hispanic residents, since they shopped and sought their entertainment in West Dallas, there was little interaction with the white population. Hispanic residents lived and attended public school in south Irving or were students at St. Luke's Catholic School but were rarely seen by white proprietors.[3]

At the same time that Irving was undergoing transformation, our neighbors in Latin America also began to experience change in many ways that would affect their lives. Due to problems abroad, the United States attempted to improve foreign relations, especially with those nations in closer proximity. The Good Neighbor Policy championed by the Hoover Administration and later the Roosevelt Administration encouraged goodwill in Latin America. In 1936, during the first visit of an American president to Argentina at the Pan American Conference, Roosevelt addressed the issue of collective security. By the late 1940s, the United States had completed agreements with every country except Argentina. Eventually, relations did change in the 1950s as the U.S. image began to change in Latin America, until John F. Kennedy began the "Alliance for Progress," and created the Peace Corps. However, corrupt governments were still a problem all over Latin America, which caused interest in coming to America. The Immigration Act of 1965 signed by Lyndon B. Johnson was not kind to Latin America. The National Origins Act of 1924 had placed no limit on immigrants from the Western Hemisphere and now Congress took action with the new act to limit the numbers to 120,000 annually, worried that the political and economic climate would lead to a surge in immigration.

Congress was correct. A population movement began all over Latin America that continues today. Civil wars in the 1970s that led to death squads, unruly armies, poverty, problems with neighboring countries, like in the case of Honduras and Nicaragua, political corruption, drug cartels, unemployment, and lack of social justice started driving thousands of Latinos away from their homes. The Immigration Act of 1990 was signed into law by President George Bush. Fortunately, the Immigration Act of 1990 provided a major revision of the use of preference put forth in the Immigration Act of 1965. It used a flexible cap based on employment and underrepresented countries. It also included family-sponsored immigration. The Act allowed undocumented Salvadorans with temporary protective status as well as nationals from designated countries that could experience armed conflict. Family members were also allowed to stay temporarily. Numbers of Latinos in Irving increased dramatically after 1990. In 1980, Irving listed a population of 109,943; of these 8,107 or 7.4 percent were described as being of Spanish origin. Twenty years later, the Census showed that Irving had 191,615 residents. Hispanics/Latinos were 59,838 or 31.2 percent; 42,318 or 22.1 percent were of Mexican origin; Puerto Ricans were 679 or 0.4 percent; Cubans were 272 or 0.1 percent; and 16,569 or 8.6 percent were other Latinos.[4] Who were these people? Why did they come here and what did they want?

Victor Rojas was 18 when he came illegally from El Salvador in the mid-1980s to Irving. Victor was born in 1960; consequently, he grew up with civil war all around his home. Fortunately, since the farm was away from the city, they could hear the gun shots but thankfully never had to deal with the guerrillas. He speaks in the interview about wanting a better future. Both of his parents had passed away and he was living on the farm with his 12 siblings. His job was to feed the cows and eventually was forced to quit school. His dream was to have his grandchildren attend college and have a good career and not live paycheck to paycheck. Victor worked in construction and sent his money back to his siblings in El Salvador to help with the farm. He met and married the second girl he ever dated, and had two children. Victor believed strongly that if he had stayed in El Salvador, his life would have been very different; in the United States, although it was tough, there were more opportunities. Victor also believed that his children benefitted from living in the United States, as did his siblings who had chosen to come to this country.[5]

Raul Maldonado, an immigrant of Puerto Rico, is also a Vietnam veteran. His journey to Irving was very different compared to others. One of nine children, he grew up and worked on his parents' farm, went to school, and did finish high school. Raul would later acquire an engineering degree while in government service and did marry before going to Vietnam. He did two tours in Vietnam, one in 1966 and another in 1969; his highest rank was Master Sergeant. Former Master Sergeant Maldonado worked covert missions and therefore did not feel comfortable giving details about his unclassified duties. When asked what music reminded him the most of Vietnam, his response was country/western tunes. In Vietnam, his pastime was writing and reading letters. Unlike so many, Raul came home to a happy home life and in 2007 when the interview was recorded had been married to his wife for 50 years. After Vietnam, Maldonado chose to come to Irving, and began working with the Federal Bureau of Investigation.[6]

Guatemala provided a hard life for Hugo Orellana. He was born in Guatemala City in 1961 to a poor family. When asked about the economic status of his family, his response was, "they were poor, just enough to make it by, not comfortable, the poor always remain poor and struggle financially." These circumstances never changed for the family. His parents, mostly his mother, taught him to respect others as well as religion, how to clean, cook, and buy groceries, and he went to the 10th grade in school. His dream was to be an automotive mechanic; however, he took a job as a police officer for $500–600 a month, which was not enough, so he made kites and sold them at the local market. He finally left Guatemala and came here illegally at 21 years of age where he has built a better life. He spends his time alone in a squeaky clean house, never eats out, and saves his money. He was not close to his father who was an assassin for the Guatemalan government, has problems showing affection, and is not close to the rest of his family who still live in Guatemala.[7]

Jose Pabst was born in the middle of a revolution in Nicaragua. The entire family, including his grandmother, lived together. Jose remembered he was especially close to his cousin Fruto. His parents were strong Catholics who taught Jose grammar and writing. When asked about his family's financial status, his response was that "they lived on a financial roller coaster." His parents came first to the United States and sent money for his expenses. Jose did not have any role models growing up; he commented in the interview that "his mother could only find work in a restaurant and he did not want to learn from those around him." Today, Jose has a Bachelor of Science and a Master's degree in Business Administration from Purdue University. Jose lives a comfortable life and knows that if he had not come to the United States, he would not have achieved his educational goals. He believes he is experiencing the American Dream at its best and loves the United States.[8]

Jonathan Galvan came from Colombia with another family. In Colombia, they lived with the extended family, so it was financially easier for the group. He went to school and graduated, and went to college for two years. In Colombia, he worked at a cell phone company but only earned enough to survive. He finally decided to speak to his parents about coming to the United States for a better life and freedom from the turmoil of his own community. In his interview, he discusses the dangers of encountering not only the guerrillas but also the corrupt police. Jonathan's father was a Pastor at the time and a target in a primarily Catholic country.[9]

Of the people mentioned in this essay, over half had to make the perilous journey from their countries to the United States. Like the Mexican illegal immigrants, Central Americans turned to coyotes to bring them to America. The cost for each traveler was $5000 with half being paid up front. It did not matter the age of the individual, it was still $5000 for each. The journey could take weeks, maybe even a couple of months. Traveling at night, in jam-packed vehicles that were not in the best condition and had no air conditioning could be a challenging experience. It was safer to go through Belize to avoid the authorities, which was also a very dangerous drive.

One of the interviewees remembered that when he, at the age of 11, and his younger brother aged 7 came alone, they had a terrible accident in Belize. Riding in a large van with over 19 people in it, the vehicle was hard to maneuver especially in heavy rain. The van went off the edge and rolled over and pinned a couple of people. At age 11, he was terrified having never seen a deceased person and did not know what to do; someone dragged him to a tree where he passed out. When he woke up, he could not find his brother. He remembered crying incessantly knowing that his mother had made him promise never to leave his brother alone. Now, he had lost his brother.

Then he heard someone calling his name and realized his brother had brought back help to look for him so that they could continue their journey. Their trip to the U.S. border took much longer since they had no money and the coyote had disappeared after the accident. Although they were able to finally reach their parents, they had very little money to send as they had exhausted their resources. Their uncle met them at the border and took them to Houston where they lived for over a decade until their parents came to the United States and brought them to Irving.[10]

In 2000, Latinos in Irving had not started establishing businesses outside of the flea markets and bazaars. Fiesta and other Hispanic grocery stores still focused more on Mexican items rather than the Latino needs. Women, much like back home, worked in the flea markets and bazaars where dishware, spices, handmade flowers, beads, clay and wooden flutes, and musical items were the most popular products. Latinos worked in the service industries and did day labor. Today, Latinos have a strong presence in the construction industries and the women are working in hair and nail salons. Both males and females can be found in the restaurant industry. Salvadoran restaurants are popular places and there are a couple of Nicaraguan and Honduran eating establishments in Irving. There are also other businesses such as check cashing, money grams, or phone card establishments.

Latinos are Catholics, but a large segment of Irving's Latinos are Pentecostal. Latinos for the most part marry within their own group or Mexicans but will rarely marry someone from another Central American country. They encourage their children to get an education and strive for the American Dream.[11] Many Latinos celebrate religious holidays and practice the same traditions as Mexican descent Catholics, such as *compadrazco*. Godparents play an important role in the raising of a child and can often have a say-so in important life decisions.

They also celebrate saints, such as El Divino Salvador del Mundo (August 1–6), a Salvadoran tradition. The Immaculate Conception (December 8) in Nicaragua is another example of a Holy day. Day of the Dead in November is best known as a Mexican holiday, but it is celebrated all over Central America. Las Posadas is practiced in Mexico and throughout Central America. Las Posadas is a nine-day observance from December 16 to 24, where nightly, families recreate Mary and Joseph's holy pilgrimage. Mother's Day is another tradition that is special to Latinos and celebrated in May. Then there is Father's Day in June, also a tradition in Latin America. September 15 is Independence Day for El Salvador, Costa Rica, Guatemala, Honduras, and Nicaragua. Latinos do not have the city-wide celebrations Mexicans have for September 16 or Cinco de Mayo; their numbers are not large enough. However, they do have block parties and small fiestas at local parks. They also gather at their homes. Often times, they move from home to home to celebrate in a day.

Latino youth in Irving are also involved in gang activity that originated in their own countries. Three that were mentioned by the gang unit are MS13, MARA, and *Salvaturcha*, all from Central America. There is significant rivalry between these gangs who are spillovers from Dallas. Members are under the age of 20 and involved in drugs and prostitution. The gang unit in Irving is very active and has been able to stop the other gangs from gaining a foothold in Irving, which is a great accomplishment because the Central American gangs are very well organized and have much money.[12]

In conclusion, this population movement has not skipped a beat. In 2014, Irving had a population of 232,406. Of these, 89,561 are listed as Hispanics and are 40.6 percent of the population. The breakdown is as follows: people of Mexican origin are 64,625 or 29.3 percent; Puerto Ricans are 1,436 or 0.7 percent; Cubans are 503 or 0.2 percent; and other Latinos number 22,997 or 10.4 percent of the Irving population.[13] As documented in the interviews in this essay, Latino immigrants come here for a better life and to leave civil war, poverty, hunger, and death. None of them have become wealthy but have still been successful in building a more positive future. They love the United States and the city of Irving and have contributed much to the social fabric of our community.

Notes

1. *Norma Stanton, Irving, Texas: From Rail to Wings, 1903–2003*, pp. 7–41 (Donning Company Publishers, 2003); Joe Rice, *Irving: A Texas Odyssey* (Northridge, CA: Windsor Publications, 1989); Ruby Caster Taylor Oral History, Ruby Caster Taylor to Yolanda Romero, February 12, 2003, at Irving, Texas (Irving, TX: Irving Archives); Catherine Schulze Oral History, Catherine Schulze to Yolanda Romero, January 9, 2003, at Irving, Texas (Irving, TX: Irving Archives); Charles Schulze Oral History, Charles Schulze to Yolanda Romero, January 9, 2003, at Irving, Texas (Irving, TX: Irving Archives).

2. Franco Oral History, Francisco Franco to Yolanda Romero, June 28, 2004, at Irving, Texas (Irving, TX: Irving Archives); Tino Soto Oral History, Tino Soto to Yolanda Romero, July 2, 2004, at Irving, Texas (Irving, TX: Irving Archives); Luis Ponce Oral History, Luis Ponce to Yolanda Romero, November 8, 2004, at Irving, Texas (Irving, TX: Irving Archives); Roy Santoscoy Oral History, Roy Santoscoy to Yolanda Romero, September 18, 2003, at Irving, Texas (Irving, TX: Irving Archives); Vincent Santoscoy Oral History, Vincent Santoscoy to Yolanda Romero, September 16, 2002, at Irving, Texas (Irving, TX: Irving Archives); Beatrice Ponce Oral History, Beatrice Ponce to Yolanda Romero, July 1, 2002, at Irving, Texas (Irving, TX: Irving Archives); Pablo Fernandez Oral History, Pablo Fernandez to Yolanda Romero, October 31, 2002, at Irving, Texas (Irving, TX: Irving Archives).

3. Franco Oral History, Francisco Franco to Yolanda Romero, June 28, 2004, at Irving, Texas (Irving Archives, Irving Francisco, Texas); Tino Soto Oral History, Tino Soto to Yolanda Romero, July 2, 2004, at Irving, Texas (Irving, TX: Irving Archives); Luis Ponce Oral History, Luis Ponce to Yolanda Romero, November 8, 2004, at Irving, Texas (Irving, TX: Irving Archives); Roy Santoscoy Oral History, Roy Santoscoy to Yolanda Romero, September 18, 2003, at Irving, Texas (Irving, TX: Irving Archives); Vincent Santoscoy Oral History, Vincent Santoscoy to Yolanda Romero, September 16, 2002, at Irving, Texas (Irving, TX: Irving Archives); Beatrice Ponce Oral History, Beatrice Ponce to Yolanda Romero, July 1, 2002, at Irving, Texas (Irving, TX: Irving Archives); Pablo Fernandez Oral History, Pablo Fernandez to Yolanda Romero, October 31, 2002, at Irving, Texas (Irving, TX: Irving Archives.); African Americans were segregated in the community of Bear Creek close to the site of one of the oldest freedmen's cemetery in Texas. Attorney Robert Powers went to court to argue on behalf of the African American community maintaining in court that they should be allowed to live in Irving.

4. Bureau of the Census, United States, 1980, 2000; City of Irving Population Records, 1980, City Hall, Irving, Texas.

5. Victor Rojas, Sr. Oral History, Victor Rojas, Sr. to Victor Rojas, Jr., April 28, 2005, at Irving, Texas, Special Oral History Collection, Yolanda Romero, Irving, Texas.

6. Raul Maldonado Oral History, Raul Maldonado to Yasmeen Maldonado Drumm, April 29, 2007, at Irving, Texas, Special Oral History Collection, Yolanda Romero, Irving, Texas.

7. Hugo Orellana Oral History, Hugo Orellana to Tommy Orellana, May 5, 2007, at Irving, Texas, Special Oral History Collection, Yolanda Romero, Irving, Texas.

8. Jose Pabst Oral History, Jose Pabst to Glenda Pabst, May 5, 2007, at Euless, Texas, Special Oral History Collection, Yolanda Romero, Irving, Texas.

9. Jonathan Galvan Oral History, Jonathan Galvan to Arthur Galvan, November 27, 2005, at Irving, Texas, Special Oral History Collection, Yolanda Romero, Irving, Texas.

10. Victor Rojas, Sr. Oral History, Victor Rojas, Sr. to Victor Rojas, Jr., April 28, 2005, at Irving, Texas, Special Oral History Collection, Yolanda Romero, Irving, Texas; Hugo Orellana Oral History, Hugo Orellana to Tommy Orellana, May 5, 2007, at Irving, Texas, Special Oral History Collection, Yolanda Romero, Irving, Texas.

11. Census, Bureau of the Census, U.S. Government, 2014.

12. Interview with Gang Unit, December 11, 2015, notes in possession of the author.

13. Census, Bureau of the Census, U.S. Government, 2014.

Contributors

Brett Bodily, PhD, Professor of English, North Lake College
Brett currently teaches writing and literary studies at North Lake College in Irving, Texas. As a researcher, he seeks to understand the human condition through qualitative methods, capturing the storied lives of adult learners striving to create a sustainable world. His professional and personal interests include homesteading, organic gardening, and culinary possibilities. He enjoys teaching yoga, attending theatre productions, and exploring photography. His passion for horses has led him to explore nonconventional means of building relationships with horses, especially his three horses at home. Because he loves all things dairy, he is currently saving up for his own cow.

James Duran, MA, Professor of Government, North Lake College
Born in El Paso, Texas, James completed his BA in Anthropology at the University of Houston, and then satisfied the MA requirements in Political Science from Texas State University. He moved to North Texas in 2012. In 2014, he was invited to serve as a co-advisor for the Student Government Association and Enactus. He joined the Sustainable Blazer Committee, Sustainability Awareness and Global Education, and the Faculty Association in 2015. *Academic mission:* To evaluate political activity of governing system(s) at all levels; identify solutions to issues deemed socially unacceptable; and encourage students to make a positive difference in their community.

Brandon Morton, Adjunct Professor of Biology, North Lake College
Brandon Morton is the sustainability coordinator and an Adjunct Professor of Biology at North Lake College in Irving, Texas. Brandon is a Dutch-American and a recognized international professional with expertise in ecology, energy, and natural resource management. He earned his Bachelor of Science in Biology from University of North Texas, where he also cofounded the sustainability program. He and his family reside in Dallas, Texas.

Yolanda Romero, PhD, Professor of History, North Lake College
Yolanda Romero was a Professor of History at North Lake College in Irving, Texas. She received her PhD in History in 1993 from Texas Tech University. An expert in Mexican American studies, her latest publications include "Adelante Compañeros: The Sanitation Worker's Struggle in Lubbock, Texas, 1968–1972" in *Texas Labor History Anthology* edited by J. K. Maroney (College Station, TX: Texas A & M University Press, 2013) and entries in the *Tejano Handbook of Texas* (Texas State Historical Association, 2015). Dr. Romero passed away in August 2016. She is dearly missed by her family, friends, students, and colleagues, yet her legacy lives on.

Roy Vũ, PhD, Professor of History, North Lake College

Roy Vũ is a Professor of History at North Lake College in Irving, Texas. He earned his PhD in History in 2006 from the University of Houston. His recent publications include "Turbulent Seas" in *Sugar and Rice Magazine*, Issue 2 (2014), edited by David Leftwich, and "Natives of a Ghost Country: The Vietnamese in Houston and Their Construction of a Postwar Community" in *Asian Americans in Dixie: Race and Migration in the South* (University of Illinois Press, 2013), edited by Khyati Y. Joshi and Jigna Desai. He and his wife, Ngọc, reside in Irving, Texas.

www.ingramcontent.com/pod-product-compliance
Lightning Source LLC
Chambersburg PA
CBHW050527280326
41932CB00014B/2480